# SATHYA
# SAI
# PARENTING

by

**Rita Bruce**

PRASANTHI NILAYAM

## Sri Sathya Sai Books & Publications Trust

PRASANTHI NILAYAM P.O. 515 134
ANANTAPUR DISTRICT, ANDHRA PRADESH, INDIA
Grams: BOOK TRUST  Phone: 87375, 87236
STD: 0855    ISD:0091-8555 Fax: 87236

ISBN NO:81-7208-283-5

First Edition May 2001

Price: Rs; 40

Published by:

**The Convenor,**
**Sri Sathya Sai Books & Publications Trust**
Prashaanthi Nilayam, India- Pin Code 515 134
Grams: BOOKTRUST STD: **08555** ISD:**0091-8555**
Telephones: **87375 . 87236**
Fax: **87236**

*Printed by:*
   *PRINT PARK*
   *No.284,1st Main, 407 SFS, Yelahanka New Town*
   *Bangalore-560 065*
   *Phone-(080) 8460784, 8563607*
   *e-mail-printpark@ mail city.com*

# TABLE OF CONTENTS

*We offer this book
to the Divine Lotus Feet
of our Beloved Sai Baba
with Love and Humility.*

*"Above all, realise that children are precious treasures.
Yours is the great task of helping them up to become
devoted servants of God and sincere aspirants of the
spiritual path."*

*Discourse 5/19/62*

# INTRODUCTION

This book is for students, young adults, married couples, parents and grandparents. It is about the *"Restoration of The Family Home"*. The strong winds of *changing values*, these external elements, have worn and torn tirelessly at the construction of family life and it needs to be repaired.

To remodel our home will take work, and we will first need to remove the decayed weakened structure and replace it with a stronger, newer edifice. To begin, we will need a floorplan to remodel our Family Home which has been designed by our architect, Sai Baba. His Divine Blueprint, His Teachings, are incorporated throughout the structure of this book helping us in a "Step by Step - How To do" method.

He places in our hands the tools and skills that are needed for remodeling the "Home of Family Values". Sai

I

Baba says, *"No one has any common sense, today."* This book attempts to restore common sense by offering practical ideas that can change our parenting skills easily.

The teachings of Sai Baba on parenting, embodying His dharmic wisdom, are the most spiritually correct methods on how to teach Human Values to our children for the purpose of building character with love, understanding and discipline.

The issues that are discussed in this book are the key issues that parents have defined in our Sathya Sai parenting workshops. Discipline is the big issue, our children are out of control and we need to correct this problem.

Sai Baba says, *"Ninety percent of the blame for spoiling the behavior and character of children, go to the parents. They show too unintelligent affection and give too indiscriminate a freedom to them."* SS January 1994 pg. 24

Another major issue is the immoral influence coming into our homes from the television, internet, and video games. The media is bringing inferior values into our homes and shaping the character of our children. This outside influence is penetrating all homes, thus peer pressure and parent pressure to comply with the values of others is powerful. Parents need a strong support system to combat the war on immorality.

This book includes Sai Baba's teachings on parenting issues, as well as scientific research that is now available supporting some major teachings of Sai Baba concerning parenting. The scientific community through recent research states a strong case for devotees to change. They need to implement different parenting techniques, and this research can help with explanations to their children, relatives and friends.

II

For example, television. "More importantly, several investigators (Healy 1990, Pearce 1992, Buzzell 1998, Winn 1985) have drawn attention to the actual act of viewing television as even more insidious and potentially damaging to the brain of the developing child than the actual content of what's on TV."

The importance of mothers staying at home is now proven with the recent studies on the early brain development of a child. Scientists have discovered that there are special "Learning Windows" which are critical time tables for our children to learn certain skills. Whenever possible I have included research along with many of Sai Baba's quotations.

This book will strengthen your reasons for a forcible parenting style. Your children are His children requiring that we teach and shape their character into mature adults who will learn and understand the nature of their own divinity, as well as the purpose of serving mankind with love. The children are His instruments to help with His Mission to create a society based on Truth, Peace, Right Conduct, Love and Non-violence.

You will also find some of the history of the women's movement in this past century. It is important to understand the major transition in the role of women that we have experience in the last fifty years, so we can move forward, further defining and refining our role as women according to Sai Baba teachings. It is indeed thrilling to be a woman in this new century. The confusion and often ungraceful behavior of women in our past and present society can be viewed as necessary steps to climb to new spiritual heights.

The story of the birth of this book called Sathya Sai Parenting started many years ago, through my lifetime career as a wife, mother and now grandmother. Swami uses every experience we have in life to its fullest fruition.

Family life has been my profession. I have been married for 44 years, had 4 children and now 6 grandchildren. My interest and investment was on the stock of making a marriage that had complications, succeed. Realizing the enormous influence our relationship had on our children and each other, became almost an obsession with me.

I asked many questions. What happened to the love that we had before marriage? Why are we so opposite? Is there any way to change behavior when it is so deeply ingrained within us? What is my role as a woman? Does society only value a woman with a career? Is motherhood only recognized as a job for those who are uneducated? What worked for my parents, why is it not working for me? The list grew, the answers were few until I met Sai Baba.

Most of Baba's teachings, I viewed and reviewed from the perspective and role of a wife and mother. I use His example as my divine parent, for the role model I should imbibe as a parent to my children. Similarly, the children can learn about the divine parent, God, through their relationship with us.

Swami says, *"Only the Atma is permanent and eternal. In fact, the Atma is the real mother. It is not proper on your part to forget this Divine Mother. Children can understand the meanings of the word fox or dog only when they see their pictures. Similarly, it is only after seeing the parents that one can understand the existence of God. When you love and respect your parents, only then you can understand the love of the Divine Parents."* SS June 1999 pg. 142

I used everything I learned about spirituality from Him, to help me improve myself and my relationship with my spouse and children. Mistakes were unavoidable as I learned about the true characteristics of a woman, wife and mother. Swami cleared my vision at a time when the world was confusing the roles of male and female.

Some people who read Sai Baba's teachings are interested in the similarity of His life with that of Jesus, others in His teachings on the Vedas, or the Gita, others in His Miracles etc., etc. We all have our own individual focus and path to spirituality. My lure was spirituality in the family.

About two years ago, a devotee asked Swami if we could give workshops in her country. Swami said, "Yes". Dr. Michael Goldstein then confirmed this with Sai Baba. Then Sai Baba gave us two interviews to talk about the workshops. I asked Swami, "If we are not here in Prasanthi to ask for Your permission, Lord, what should we do?" He replied, "You go wherever you are asked. Swami will Bless; this is Swami's work."

Swami said, *"The home, too, must feel the change in the child's behavior. It may be advisable to gather the parents together and give them guidelines on childcare, and on the higher ideals of family and social life."* SSS 10, pgs. 207 - 208

For ten years prior to giving workshops, we have given talks on Sai Baba's teachings on Marriage and Parenting at Conferences and Centers. Then in 1996, we began giving an 8 hour workshop on Sathya Sai Marriage and an 8 hour workshop on Sathya Sai Parenting.

Moms and dads kept requesting that I write a book synthesizing my ideas on parenting with Sai Baba's teachings of human values. Repeatedly, they told us how much they needed help.

Brother Jagadeeshan, at the First Overseas Convention of Chair Persons in November, 1998, asked this question. "How many of you know the 9 points of conduct?" Many hands went up. Then he asked, "How many of you will come up here and recite them?" About 4 hands went up out of 1000 delegates. It gave us the opportunity to face what we think we know versus what we really know.

I too would like to pose some questions concerning Sai Baba's teachings on marriage and parenting. What does Swami say is the primary responsibility of parents? What does He say about Divorce? What are the roles, nature and virtues of a man and woman? What is the purpose of marriage? Why is discipline important to teach our children? If a child does not listen to you, what does Swami advise us to do? These questions are important for us to know, and yet how many devotees can answer them?

We often assume that parents are well prepared, but are they in reality? Most parents are burdened with both having to hold paying jobs, in addition to the full time work of family life. Time is scarce and exhaustion is the theme. Swami's teachings on marriage and parenting are not in the form of one discourse, but woven into the texts of many different discourses. This is very time consuming for parents to read, in an already crammed and often stressful time-frame. The reality is that most devotees are not familiar with Sai Baba's teaching on Marriage and Parenting.

Sai says, *"Parents do not correct the children. That should not be so. One has to be strict with the children. The Elders need to go through 'Human Values' and teach this to the children."* Swami's Talks to the Students

In every country, irrespective of their culture, when we speak on the topics of Sai Baba's teachings on Marriage and Parenting, we hear the same plea: "We need more programs like this."

Is it any wonder when we know that 50% of all marriages are ending in divorce; when we see the family unit disintegrating into singles; when we see babies being left at the day care centers before they are 8-weeks old; when we see children coming home to an empty nest? Few have the needed patience to work with a child after a stressful exhausting day. How can "Quality Time" compare with "All The Time"? Is there a need within the Sai Family for education on parenting? The answer must be an emphatic and definite **YES.**

We are training the Sai Spiritual Education Teachers, who are working with the children 1 or 2 hours a week in class, and if the parents are not enforcing what is being taught by the teachers, the balance between theory and application is lost, along with the unity of thought, word and deed. Common sense tells us that the parents who shoulder the greatest responsibility for the child's development also need help.

Sai says, *"For lakhs of students and children who go to school, the mother is the first teacher."* SS Dec. 1996 pg. 334

Parents garner needed support from each other when they talk about their mutual problems in the workshops.

They realize that they are not alone, and in their small groups, they find solutions to the problems that confront them. We give handouts of Swami's Quotes on many issues concerning parenting, and they are grateful to Swami who gave them this opportunity. One father said, "To realize that the solutions to these problems are within us, was an important aspect of this workshop." One father said to another father, "I've known you for years, but we have never talked like this!"

You see Swami's children are unique because from birth they are taught and often exposed to God in form on earth. The worldly values and methods of raising children are light years away from what Swami expects. How can these children become instruments in His Divine Mission without a healthy combination of love and discipline?

Devotees need materials that will help them become Sai parents, such as this book. They also need the workshops that give them the opportunity, the time and the format to discuss the problems that are thrust upon them from the uncensored, negative influences in our world.

Another support system for parents would be a parent study group in the Sai Centers. The family needs to be strengthened. Today, the entire family structure is in crisis. These steps will arm the parents with new tools that will improve and strengthen their family.

Swami said in our interview, *"The Young Adults should have the same program on Marriage and Parenting as the married couples."*

Swami does not want the future generation to make the same mistakes that we have made. Many of our young adults obtain University Degrees and yet not a single class have they attended on marriage and parenting. Where is the training? Generation upon generation pass the skills, whether good or not so good, to the next generation without being taught how to improve their family life. What happens to us in our childhood, influences us throughout our life. **Nothing has such a profound effect on our life; and yet we are unprepared.** It is quintessential that this be corrected in the Sai Family.

Why is there a lack of moral education on Marriage and Parenting? Why has this crucial issue slipped through the cracks in our society? Motherhood has been a job that few desired because it has been so little valued. There is no glamour or pay in this job, only sacrifice.

Young adults are the future leaders of the Sai Organization and the future parents of the souls that Swami will send to them; Sai Education in marriage and parenting provides the needed tools to help solve their problems as they arise. This is the object of this book! To offer a tool to help prepare and familiarize parents and future parents with the teaching of Sai Baba on Family Values

Education for parents and young adults is pivotal in strengthening the family, and when we rivet ourselves to the Love of Sai, this will forge and encouraging the link of togetherness. We must make the effort and He will provide the Grace to harmonize and spiritualize our marriage and parenting skills.

He says, *"The home and the family is the basic social institution everywhere in the world. When the home improves, the whole world will be better."*

# CHAPTER 1
## GOD'S CHILDREN OR OURS?

**M**y *husband, my wife, my children, who is this* **MY**? asks Sai Baba. How easy it is to claim ownership. From the moment that we see the creation of our child, we forget that it is God's child. The attachment begins. We commence with who does the child look like? Oh! The eyes look like the father's and the mouth looks like the mother's and the hair is grandmother's etc. It is glorious to see this child of "ours", and immediately we start admiring OUR creation.

As the days progress, the child becomes more and more our extension. It becomes our center of attention, in every waking moment. Every person that enters a room where a baby is present, stops, turns, admires and is secretly enchanted. A mere infant, can cast a captivating spell. As a mother I have often felt this with reverence.

While the days, months and years grow, so does the attachment. The distinction between "God's" or "my" child becomes steadily blurred. In our blindness, we forget the reality of who is the parent? We or God?

Sai offers an alternative: *"Parents must feel that they are servants appointed by the Lord to tend the little souls that are born in their households, as the gardener tends the trees in the garden of the Master.* SSS 1 pg. 70

From the time that a child is born, their physical well-being rests in their parents hands. They are depending on you for their food, warmth, safety, cleanliness, etc. How fragile is their existence without someone to watch over them continuously. We are all aware that God and His guardian angels watch over our children, but we are the physical guardians that God has selected to foster and care for His child.

Sai says, *"First and foremost, you should show gratitude to your parents, love them and respect them. Your blood, your food, your head, your money are all the gifts of your parents. You do not receive these gifts directly from God. All that is related to God is only indirect experience. It is only the parents who you can see directly and experience their love. So, consider your parents as God."* SS June 1999 pg. 141

We are the foster parents of God's children. We simply are playing a role, not a simple role but an extremely valuable one. But, if we confuse ourselves with the attitude of "ownership" we may loose sight of the purpose for which the child was given.

Swami says, *"Parents have the primary responsibility to mold the character of their children."*

We become so attached to our child that we find it sometimes impossible to mould their character. We would rather be their friend. It's nicer and often easier to be their friend. They will like us if we are their friend. It's much more difficult to be their parent. They don't like us when we tell them what to do. We can identify with this because we don't like to be told what to do. We cannot confuse this issue. The rules are distinctively different for children. They need to be told what to do because for the time being, you are their conscience. Theirs is not developed as yet.

Our children, want us to take care of them and provide for their every need, but more than that today, they want us to provide for their every desire. This is acceptable to them but they find it unacceptable when you are correcting their behavior. They want you to be their parents when you are providing for their physical needs and desires, but they do not want you to be their parents when it becomes necessary to correct their behavior. They want to be spoiled, pampered, have their own way. Just don't tell them what to do! The question to be asked is, "Who is controlling who?"

And this is the problem that we as parents are confronted with more often than we would like to admit. We know what is best for them, but they do not want to hear it. Therefore conflict ensues, and as you know this can start at a very early age. The young toddler who wants to walk on a table, or jump on the bed, or eat sweets before dinner, or throw food in the air rebels at an early age.

Sai says, *"The parents themselves are not competent to guide the children; they dote on them and do not know how to correct them, they themselves have reprehensible habits and ways of life."* SSS #9 pg. 1

God is our Parent; He is the Conscience within, and we as foster parents assume the same role for our children. God has entrusted this human soul into our hands for us to love, cherish, and discipline. Character development is difficult, because your conscience must be your child's until theirs is strongly established.

How many times have we noticed the amount of time that our dear Swami spends with His students? And how many times have we heard Him speak about our children being the future leaders of the world? The souls that Sai Baba gives to devotees are highly evolved souls who need the stronger will of a mature parent. These souls are extremely aware and forceful. They can easily go astray without the strong guidance and tough love of confident loving parents.

When we examine the small number of people who presently know that God is on earth, compared to the population of the world, the ratio is daunting; there are so few. It is only common sense to reason that the souls gifted to devotees are very old souls. Sai Baba is counting on us to empower His values into their character, because they will need this strength to help him in His divine mission. Are we failing Him?

Swami says, *"If man cannot recognize the uniqueness of humanness, what is the use of taking the human birth? Among all beings, human birth is the rarest and noblest. Having got such a sacred human birth, man should turn his senses Godward from his early age."* SS May 1999 pg. 131

In this life, God incarnate has taught us Truth; let us share this Wisdom with our children. We, as parents, do not

4

have to stumble in the darkness of ignorance. We can instruct our children with Swami's teaching on Right Conduct. We need not hesitate about what is the correct method to nurture spirituality in our children. His teachings and example are quite clear. _Sai_-chology is the best form of psychology. We can instruct our children with Sai's formula of chanting God's Name and visualizing His Form, as well as, meditating on the Light, to bring Peace into their little hearts and minds. This awakens the quietness of inner life. We can instruct our children through our example as does Swami, demonstrating the ultimate gift of selfless love. Not only do we need to instruct our children, but it is extremely important that they are exposed to the same teachings from another source.

Our children need to attend Sai Spiritual Education classes. Many times they will listen and more readily accept from someone other than yourself. The Sai Spiritual Education teachers as well as Education in Human Values teachers are trained to help your child understand Sai Baba's Values: Truth, Right Conduct, Peace, Non-Violence and Love. When the parents practise and enforce these values in their home, in addition to classroom instruction, a dynamic imprint is made on your child. Most parents are not following Swami's rules for children, and the Sai Spiritual Education Classes are not getting results. The teachers can only teach, the parents need to enforce the rules.

Sai Baba says, *"The atmosphere in the home should be such that it should nourish and develop the values inculcated in the child during Sai Spiritual Education classes. Parental co-operation and encouragement are vital for the program to be effective. So often you can see the difference in a child whose parent is actively involved with the program. This interest should be encouraged by the SSE teachers, by bringing parents into the program from the very early stages, and using their skills to further enhance the children's potential. Children learn a great deal by observing and copying what their parents do. Thus it makes it imperative for parents to plant the right ideals in the minds of their children, by the example of their own conduct."* SS January 1994 pg. 24

When else in the history of mankind have parents ever had access to a more loving, wise, inspiring example of divinity than Sri Sathya Sai Baba, to teach them how to "mould the character" of another soul? What a Blessing. It is essential for us to view parenting from this higher level of consciousness, and take our responsibility seriously.

Certainly, we can recognize the uniqueness of Swami's birth; God is on earth. How often does God Incarnate on earth, and how often in our past have we had the opportunity to be here with Him?

Sai Baba told Dr. Hislop that if a soul walks away from Swami, it will take eon upon eon before that soul takes birth again. The chance of this soul coming again while God is on earth is extremely remote. These souls, our children, need to have spiritually powerful parents. They will be the soldiers of morality that will fight the battle of good against evil. Their spiritual strength is needed to push during the labor of Truth, Righteousness, Peace, Non-violence and Love on earth, the *birth of The Golden Age.*

In summary, if we clarify the issue that this is not our child but God's, it might be easier to accept Swami's teaching in the following pages on what needs to be accomplished to bring this child closer to God, and therefore more spiritually evolved than when this soul arrived in our care. It is extremely important for all of us to understand the enormity of the work at hand. The question is:

**"God has given us a jewel, do we want to give it back to Him Tarnished or Illuminated?"**

# CHAPTER 2

# SANCTIFY YOUR MARRIAGE

I t is appropriate for me to begin with the relationship of a man and woman. This book is about parenting, not marriage, but we will use this chapter to stress the importance of a good marital relationship because it is the foundation for healthy parenting.

If you are a young adult and contemplating marriage, it is paramount that you consider deeply the lifelong commitment you will need to make to your marriage partner. If you have decided to have children, you will be required to assume an even larger responsibility.

Swami speaks on the topic of marriage.

*"Today we find elaborate arrangements and gala celebrations in marriage functions. One is filled with joy when one gets married, but one does not realize that the*

9

*happiness of married life is but momentary. This is not true happiness. O mind, tell me what gives the real happiness? It is Divine proximity."* SS May 1999 pg. 134

Marriage is the first institution that God gave to mankind. It is a sacred institution, that has been reduced to a sexual institution. If you don't like one partner, hop over to the next. We are acting like animals instead of human beings, so far from our divine nature.

Even though there exist various types of relationships that are parenting children today, the structure of married couples is the one that Swami has recognized. Living together as husband and wife is acceptable to Swami, but living together, unmarried, is not. When you enter into a sexual relationship with another person who is not your marriage partner, you are disavowing the sacred institution that God gave to man.

Swami says, *"It was lust that caused the downfall of Ravana, the one of great penance and the master of 64 types of knowledge. He not only ruined himself but his whole kingdom. Without purity of heart all the spiritual practices are of no use."* Ladies Day Discourse 11\19\98

What happens is this: you are enjoying the pleasure of the physical, mental and emotional bodies of each other without the lifetime commitment to be responsible for helping one another in good times as well as bad. The risk of your vulnerability is high. Lack of commitment means that one or both partners are not fully present with their whole available beings, both living fully and courageously.

Both are hedging their pledge, as well as their benefits. When you hold back to reduce discomfort, you also limit the benefits of a shared life of remarkable transformation. You are sharing God's precious gift of your bodies, but are you fully sharing the other aspects of yourselves: your minds, hearts, and will, your hopes and fears, your sorrows and joys? What happens when one partner is all there and the other isn't? When the relationship is over, one or both may be seriously wounded mentally, emotionally, spiritually, or even physically. Some people carry the wounding with them forever.

Swami says, *"Before marriage, he is half body. Before marriage, she is half body. Lady is always left side. Right side is gent's. The gent's body is always the right side of the wife. Now you have only one body. Wife before marriage is half body. Now the left side is joined with the right side and you are full body."* Vision of Sai I pg. 129

When we live together unmarried, and one partner decides to leave the other, it is radical surgery separating two halves that were joined as one. There is usually one person who will be ready to leave a relationship, and one that will not. The one that is not ready is very hurt. The mental, emotional, physical and spiritual scars are left behind like dead carnage in the conscious and sub-conscious mind.

Swami says, *"Marriage means your life, a whole lifetime together, not just a few days or a few weeks, or a few years."* Golden Age pg. 145

We are sending the wrong signals to our young. The young adults are very concerned that they will not find a partner who will make this lifetime commitment. It is an ever growing fear. They sometimes think that the answer is to live with someone before they get married, to find out if they are compatible. And if you find out that you are not compatible, what are you going to do? Dump the undesirable?

Sai Baba says, *"Just as woman should consider one person and one person only as her husband, man too has to be faithful to one woman and one woman only, as his mate, his wife."* "Wife Memorandum" by Jagadeesan

Am I speaking too strongly? Yes. But isn't the divorce and infidelity rate overwhelming and isn't our immoral behavior being accepted as normal by our young? This is exactly what is happening in our society. People are hurting. They are coming to Swami in droves because they feel so unloved. This very situation of sleeping around can lead to low self-esteem as well as feelings of rejection or abandonment. First we're loved; then we're not. I remember playing this game as a child.

You pick a flower and start tearing off the petals one by one saying, "He loves me; He loves me not." Whatever petal remains supposedly reveals whether or not my boyfriend loves me . The story pictures how little by little we are tearing each other apart.

Swami says, *"You are really loving yourself, for there is only you in everyone. He is I. Whoever you injure, it is you that suffer; whomsoever you cheat, it is you that are cheated. There are no others. You are all living cells in the body of God. You are yourself, God"*. Vision of Sai I pg. 129

In America, in 1997 according to Vital Statistics Report, Vol 46, No. 12, 49% of marriages ended in divorce. For every two marriages there is now one divorce - a tripling of the divorce rate between 1960 and 1980. (US Department of Commerce, Bureau of the Census, "Current Population Reports," October 1981.)

Swami said to us, "In America, they are coming, one woman one year, and another woman the next. Swami never knows who they are coming with." He also said, "His children, fighting with her children, fighting with their children."

Yes, there are circumstances that warrant separation. Swami says this:

*" Mira was chanting the name of Lord Krishna and her mind was filled with the thoughts of Krishna. But, her husband thought that she was crossing her limits in the name of devotion to Krishna. So, one day, he threw her out of the temple for the sake of false worldly honor. Then she wrote a letter to Tulsidas seeking his advice as to what she should do, whether to give up Krishna, the eternal companion, or to forsake her husband. Tulsidas sent a reply saying, 'Mother, God is the greatest of all and the path leading to God is the noblest of all. Husband is like a passing cloud, but God is always with you, even before your birth and after your death. How can you give up God who is the Embodiment of Truth? Husband entered your life in the middle and will go away in the middle. You may serve him as long as he is alive. But, when he himself discards you, there is nothing wrong in leaving him for the sake of God.' It is not proper to expect the wife to suffer at the hands of a wicked husband."* SS May 1999 pg. 132

But these physical abusive relationships are the exception rather than the rule. People are leaving because they found someone they like better; they want more freedom, or in general , "they just didn't get what they wanted."

Swami says, *"The feeling of friendship and love is lacking in man today. Just as a honeybee sucks nectar from a bitter flower, so also man should be able to see good even in bad. You should be able to draw the water of happiness even from the well of misery. That is the true quality of love. Pleasure is an interval between two pains. Pleasure and pain coexist in God's creation itself."* Gurupoornima Discourse 8\3\99

We sometimes think that the reason  human love fails is  because it did not seem to produce what we want.  The question we must ask is what is the purpose of a relationship? Is  it  to fulfill our needs?  You fill my needs; and I'll fill yours.  The purpose of a relationship is not to have another who might fulfill you; but to have another with whom you might share your fulfilment.

Swami says, *"Selflessness is God. To feel mine and thine is ego. It is to kill the ego that two souls are brought together. They can learn to adjust to one another and forget their egos."* Golden Age  pg. 143

Marriage is a spiritual laboratory that provides us with the opportunity to sacrifice our desires and give to another. Our relationships are built on not what I can give, but what can I get.  This is the wrong way, says Baba.

Of course you will be constantly challenged in marriage. I personally think it is the greatest path to Self-Realization in this Kali Yuga Age.  I read this quote from a book called, "Conversations With God", pg. 115.

"It is a great challenge, this path of the householder. There are many distractions, many worldly concerns. The aesthetic is bothered by none of these. He is brought his bread and water, and given his humble mat on which to lie, and he can devote his every hour to prayer, meditation, and contemplation of the Divine. How easy to see the Divine under such circumstances! How simple a task! Ah, but give one a spouse, and children. See the Divine in a baby who needs changing at 3 AM. See the Divine in a bill that needs paying by the first of the month. Recognize the hand of God in the illness that takes a spouse, the job that's lost, the child's fever, the parent's pain. Now we are talking Saintliness."

Most will marry an opposite, of this I am certain. If one spouse color codes the file for bills, the other will use it for a beverage coaster. If one licks the envelope, the other will seal it with water. If you rarely spend money on yourself, the other will spend lavishly. If you like the checkbook balanced, the other writes without memory. If you want sweets, the other likes spicy. If you believe in a strict time schedule, the other looses time. If you like the sink cleared of dishes, the other stacks them etc., etc. Opposites attract and you also bring balance to each other.

You will notice this opposition brings friction, "ego" rubbing. Sometimes this program of opposites can drive you crazy. The question remains, "Who will sacrifice their ego?" When you live alone, there is no person with whom to disagree.

Swami tells us, *"First you must understand each other, after that adjustment will be easy. Today, 90% of people try adjustment first. This is the wrong way. First understanding. Sometimes, it is natural for you to have anger, ego, temper, tension. You must have adjustment and understanding."* Vision of Sai I pg. 129

The challenge is to understand one another and this is accomplished in two ways: first, verbal communication, second is witnessing or observation. Observation is excellent, but speaking is the best way to confirm what you have observed, because you might falsely assume an incorrect motive.

Communication is the lifeline in marriage. If it is broken, there is no understanding and then there is no adjustment. Lack of communication is the number one complaint of married couples. Marriage is dependent upon communication. We communicate so differently that it is almost impossible to understand each other without speaking to each other. Remember, you marry an opposite.

Unless we take the time to communicate our thoughts, decisions, emotions and actions, we cannot comprehend each other. When there is no understanding, we live in darkness; alone, we feel rejected and unloved. Who wants to live like this?

What prevents us from speaking the truth about our thoughts and feelings? Most of the time it is this little culprit called, ego. If we really want to know each other, then we have to open up and share what is inside of us.

The fears, the hurts, the insecurity, the faults, the problems, the mistakes are no secret; we all have them. Why hide them? We're not this body. We are simply playing a role and if in this role we are working on our karmic problems, then the sooner we get them into the light of consciousness from the darkness of the sub-consciousness, then the sooner we can help to heal each other.

Swami says, *"Today people are not making any effort to understand this principle of love. It is only the power of*

16

*love that can nullify a curse of a sin. It is only love that can remove all the bitter feelings and enhance the sweetness of life."* Gurupoornima Discourse 8\3\99

The greatest gift you can give to each other is truthful communication. Swami says, *"Understanding then adjustment."* Communication then transformation.

When Robert, my husband, and I began to place more emphasis on communication, we began with small talk. It is not easy to open yourself up, to begin speaking on a very personal level. Start slowly, advises our Lord Sai.

We began by sharing what happened to us during the day, our problems, how we solved them, or didn't solve them. We asked each other's opinion. Communicating and listening without judgment or criticism, taught us to trust each other. When we did judge, or criticize, or loose our center, we would apologize. The more we practised, the quicker came the apology if we said or did something that offended the other.

I read years ago, that if you are in a disagreement with someone, touching them in a gentle way stops the argument. This works. The touch is comforting and can stop the mouth from uttering hurtful opinions.

Sai Baba says, *"She who knows the mind of the husband and speaks softly and sweetly is the real friend. Why sometimes, when the wife has to point out the path of Dharma to the husband, she takes on the role even of a Father! When the husband is down with illness she is the Mother."* "Wife Memorandum" by Jagadeesan

It is the effort to communicate and sacrifice your wants that binds the relationship together. Throughout the process of married life, you are learning unconditional love. Working together to solve the conflicts and the problems that life presents to you is actually the adhesive that glues you together. You are sharing life with each other. God did not promise us that when we married, we would live happily ever after; **Disney World did!** It is sheer fantasy.

Swami says, *"Today, there is the tendency of separation, not coming together. Life is full of troubles and challenges. We should not separate ourselves because of these but rather face them together. Now when trouble comes, even if it is small, it separates us. That should not be the tendency, one should give one's heart to another."* Golden Age pg. 140 - 143

I realized that when Robert and I married, it was physical attraction, and not unconditional love that brought us together. A partner that is self-realized and able to give the pure unconditional love that our beloved Swami gives continuously, is a rare exception. So for most of us, marriage is the laboratory that teaches us how to remove our ego, and to share this divine love with our spouse and children.

Swami says, *"Love is life for man and love is everything in this world. It is love that shines brilliantly in every individual. But man, not being able to comprehend the significance of love attributes physical relationship to it. The love of a mother towards her child is affection. The love that exists between wife and husband is infatuation. The love that exists among friends and relations is attachment. The love towards material objects is desire. Love in totality, directed towards God is known as devotion."* Gurupoornima Discourse 8\3\99

18

My husband and I are still learning the ways of divine love. We have shared our mistakes, *mis-takes*, as Swami says. With the passage of time, I now know that our relationship was strengthened because of both the adversity and the joy that we shared. The time we invested in each other developed our relationship. There were moments in which we would disagree, get angry, want to leave, not love each other, etc., issues we all share in common. The many moods of our personalities are the building blocks for evolving character. The struggle of changing yourself and sharing what is going on inside is love.

Sai Baba says, *"In the future, husband's troubles are wife's troubles and wife's troubles become husband's. It is like, if one part of the body is paralyzed, the other part of the body feels the paralysis. And so, your wife must feel your pains and you must feel her pains. Both of your pains are removed by Swami. Both of you have Swami. Both husband should help wife and wife should help husband."* Vision of Sai I pg. 129

"Relationships are constantly challenging, constantly calling you, to create, express and experience higher and higher aspects of yourself, grander and grander visions of yourself, ever more magnificent versions of yourself. NO WHERE CAN YOU DO THIS MORE IMMEDIATELY THAN IN RELATIONSHIPS." Conversations with God pg. 122

Because we suffered, worked, and survived together, a hidden power which I call "Trust Power" evolved in our relationship. I didn't know this until years passed. Only after years of experience did we build the house that could not be blown down by the evil wind of selfishness. Because

19

of time spent with each other, enough time to test the water of living in many different circumstances, we eventually grew to understand that we would be there for each other. This, unknowingly transformed us.

This provided security for ourselves and our children. I would tell them, we are not perfect but you are learning that you can make a relationship succeed by helping each other through the ups and downs. We all want acceptance, a loving spouse, a relationship of understanding, someone to share our experience of life, but few want to work for it. They think it will happen as soon as they say, "I DO". This is just the beginning. It is a lifetime of commitment and effort. But invest these two ingredients and the Grace of the Lord will reward you with a companion for life.

If you are married and have children, separation or divorce can be a grim result for the innocent victims, the children. Psychologists say that, "Divorce is as traumatic as the death of a parent."

Sometimes death is easier for a child because there is closure. Divorce is always present, always a reminder of their parent's separation. Sometimes the children become pawns played back and forth by the opposing parents. The children hear the fights over parental rights, financial support, who's taking the child for the week-end, which parent is living with whom etc. These circumstances can be a series of continuous rejections for the child. It is often a disaster when viewed from the eyes of a child. Their immaturity cannot handle the emotional turmoil. One parent is tempted with the absence of their spouse to speak ill of the other, and to bribe the children for their affection and approval.

A teen-ager recently confided in me that she is "better off" since her parents got divorced. I asked her why? Because each parent took her places and spent more money. It is true that some of our children have more privileges, money, toys, clothes, vacations, cars, videos, telephones etc., etc., but they live in a world of divorced parents, who are shuffling the child from house to house to suit their own convenience. Sometimes they see their parents treat each other with rejection, jealousy, anger and selfishness. Is it any wonder that the values of the world are creeping into our children's behavior?

Sai Baba says, *"Due to the impact of Kali Age, people want to attain divine grace without making any effort whatsoever. Wickedness, misery and violence are on the rise because love for God is waning. Transform all your wicked qualities like jealousy and anger into love. Whatever happens in this world, consider it as an act of love."* Gurupoornima Discourse 8\3\99

Dear hearts, I know that marriage and raising children is not easy. But Swami wants us to work together to resolve our differences. You may live in what you think is an impossible situation, but if we continue to bring the light of love to our partner, Swami will help. When we stop the judging and criticism, they're less likely to blame you, especially if your behavior is becoming closer to that of a loving spouse. Just small changes in our behavior can make a large impression. If we give our spouse no reason to dislike us, then eventually they will not be able to continue blaming because their own guilt will force them to look at their own self.

Swami says, *"There is nothing that love cannot achieve in this world. It can even melt the hardest of rocks. When the principle of love in every human being is unified it becomes cosmic love. Do you want to quench your thirst for love? Yearn for His grace and worship Him. In order to experience bliss, develop love more and more. The more you develop love, the more you will experience bliss. Bliss cannot be attained without love. In fact, it is love that takes the form of bliss."* Gurupoornima Discourse 8\3\99

A healthy, loving and strong relationship between a husband and wife is the corner stone that sets the foundation on which to raise a family. Marriage, the first institution that God gave us, is a brilliant system for keeping creation intact. It is the basic unit of society.

God's system is ingenious. The family unit is designed to nourish a child with all the necessities needed to build a well balanced mind, body and spirit. It is also a symbolic house, of order against chaos: marriage is the foundation, the walls are the limits and boundary's (the rules), and the roof is the security and protection for a child. The family unit is designed by God as the structure to birth and nurture young souls, to foster their identity in a protected environment.

If we do not improve our family relationships, society will continue to deteriorate. Then what can we expect from the future generation? How can they flourish in this fear driven world? If we are going to have children then we must become responsible adults who are willing to stay together and teach their family spiritual values in an atmosphere of joy and love.

Sai says, *"That home, where the husband and the wife are bound together by holy love, where every day both are engaged in the reading of books that feed the soul, where the name of the Lord is sung and His Glory remembered, that home is really the Home of the Lord."* "Wife Memorandum" Jagadeesan

# CHAPTER 3

# LOVE GOD, FEAR SIN, GUARD HUMAN VALUES

## DIVINE DISCOURSE

*If free from arrogance, you are loved.*

*If free from anger, you are free of sorrow.*

*If free from desires, you gain wealth.*

*If free from greed, you become happy.*

(Sanskrit Shloka)

EMBODIMENTS of Love ! So long as a man is puffed up with pride, none, not even his wife and children will love him. One should shed his ego and arrogance, if he wants to be loved by others. One has to suffer grief and misery as long as he is prone to anger. It is only when he gives up anger he can be happy. So long as one goes on multiplying his desires, he will continue to be in want. When he controls his desires, man attains prosperity. Greed makes a man unhappy and miserable. Only when greed and miserliness are given up can one have an enjoyable and peaceful life.

The whole world and the objects therein are inter-related by the bond of love. It is love that binds the human race together. The world cannot exist without love. God is love and resides in the heart of every one as the embodiment of love. Based on this truth we pray, "Lokaa-Samasthaa-Sukhino Bhavanthu" (all the people in the world should be happy).

*In ancient times, the sages and saints sacrificed everything for the sake of the welfare of humanity. Even the youth of those times followed suit. They are remembered even today because of their spirit of selfless sacrifice. On the contrary, the youth of today are becoming exceedingly greedy and totally selfish and harboring feelings of hatred and jealousy, while those in the ancient times were leading a life of Thyaaga and Yoga (sacrifice and sense control). The present day youth want to lead a life of Bhoga (enjoying worldly and carnal pleasures) which results in Roga (disease).*

## Make God your friend

*On the journey of earthly life, people take some wealth for expenses and when they finish the journey and reach the goal, they hand over the balance to some trustworthy friend and sleep soundly. Everyone brings the wealth of love from the moment of his birth. In this Karmakshethra (field of activity) that is the world, it is difficult to safeguard the measure of Prema (love). Therefore, everyone should look for a faithful friend. Today, the only true friend is God. When you hand over the wealth of love to God, it will be easy for you to carry on a life of security and peace.*

*There is no greater teacher than your heart. Time is a great treacher. The world is a scriptural text. God is the great friend. With full faith in these four entities, one should lead his life on this earth. Prema (love) is the natural possession of every human being. It is the fruit of the tree of life. There are certain impediments in your enjoyment of the fruit. But, before tasting a fruit, you have to remove the skin and rind covering the pulp inside and also cast off the seed. The fruit of love is covered by the thick skin of ego. You have to peel off this skin of 'mine' and 'thine'. Then only you can taste the sweet juice. That is why the Vedas describe God as Raso Vai Sah (Supreme sweet essence).*

*By pure love, you should establish unity with the Divine. The path of Prema (love) is the straightforward road to realize the Divine. The human life is a journey from 'I' to 'We'. It is also progressing from Svam to Soham (individual self to the state of merger with the Divine).*

### Three types of Prema

*This means that everyone of your actions must be done as an offering to God. But, nowadays people start their journey from 'I' and come back to the same 'I'. This is selfishness. The day you give up selfishness you are on the right path. You experience love in three ways: Swaartha Prema (self-oriented love), Paraartha Prema (love towards all fellowbeings) and Anyonya Prema (mutual give and take type of love).*

*"I should be happy. I should enjoy all pleasures and be comfortable. I do not care for others." This is the attitude of Swaartha Prema (selfish love). Anyonya Prema represents the feeling that not only himself but also his relatives and friends should be comfortable and enjoy a good life. But, Paraartha Prema represents the feeling that all should be happy in the entire world. This is the highest type of Prema (love).*

*There are three examples to illustrate these three types of love. Spaartha or selfish love is comparable to the bulb that illumines just one single small room. This cannot be called love at all. Anyonya Prema is like moonlight. Though it illumines all directions, it is very dim. It does not help one to have a clear perception. You may mistake a rope for a serpent and a stump of wood as a human body in moonlight. Similarly, you may mistake a good man to be a wicked one and vice versa due to illusion. But Paraartha Prema is like Sunlight which is very bright and will not give room for any doubt.*

25

*The confused person will be overpowered by delusion. He may believe the words of wicked persons which may appear to be sweet. The words of wise people may appear to be unsavory but they communicate nectarine Truth. Divine love is like a downpour of rain, although sometimes interspersed with hard hailstones hurting you. But remember! They melt into the water of love for you. Similarly divinity sometimes may appear to be hurting you. But you should realize it contains nothing but love. God is love. Love is God. Live in Love. You should make an effort to lead such a life.*

## Look for your own defects

Some persons consider small defects in others as huge mistakes and criticize them while they ignore even great drawbacks in themselves. This is highly improper. The correct method is to magnify your own small mistakes and consider them as big mistakes and the big mistakes of others as small ones of no consequence. That is how you can control the commission of errors. With this attitude, you will be able to realize the Divine. The love of humans is earthly and selfish while Divine Love is spiritual and selfless. It is pure love. The ancients described the Divine as eternal, immortal, pure and unsullied. In order to experience the Love of God, you should give up petty-minded selfishness and expand your love.

Let us take an example of how the love of a newly married man to his spouse decreases as days go by. In the beginning he shows considerable concern when they are walking on the road and come across a thorn. The man shows a lot of concern and pulls the wife aside. In the same situation a few months later, he retorts, "Are you blind? Can you not see the thorn?" Thus, the worldly love will become diluted while Divine Love will be constant and steady.

People cannot understand the greatness of Divine Love. They misconstrue this love and even blame God when they do not get their low desires fulfilled. Some want liberation. What is liberation? It is liberation from desires. They want to see God. Should you not have the requisite faith and feeling in your heart for this?

### Aspire to experience Divine Love

Even when you live close to God you cannot see God unless you have the faith and devotion. Just like a frog in the pond which is ignorant of the honey in the lotus, though nearer to it. While honey bees from far off places know the existence of honey in the flower and come and taste it, people from distant lands come and experience the sweetness of God's Love, while those nearer are not able to do so.

The proximity to the Divine can elevate human to the level of the Divine. But many fail to realize this and waste their lives. Love is in everyone, but, because it is turned to selfish ends, it becomes attachment. You should aspire to experience Daivi Prema (Divine Love).

In the modern world, youth should know the nature of true love. Many from abroad mix with persons of the opposite sex, calling them boyfriend and girlfriend. If you really love each other you must get married and not continue living as friends.

A few years back, a foreign youth was sitting under a tree with a crestfallen face. He was just in his late teens, and when questioned by Swami, he said that his second wife had deserted him and he was anxiously thinking of his child she bore. If at this age he had worries, imagine what would happen when he became older? Some young people even before they are twenty years of age get married, divorced and re-marry again and get separated from wife and child too and later feel sorry for themselves. They do not realize the value of human life which is both rare and sacred.

*According to the Upanishaths, human life is sacred and rare. The human being is noble and powerful. He is called Maanava, that is, 'not new at all but eternal'. It is the body that changes often, not the Aathma (the Inner Being or Self).*

### God is the changeless Truth

*Young men and women! You may be getting a lot of thoughts because of your food and other habits. You should discriminate whether they are good or bad. You should not be carried away by bookish and superficial knowledge. You should have practical knowledge to make your life useful. Achieve coordination between your education and behavior. Perfect harmony in thought, word and deed is the hallmark of a human being. You should have full faith in God with no doubt at all. Divinity is beyond your human comprehension with the physical equipment you have. Your thoughts are only reflections, resound and reaction of the outer world. God has no such reactions. He has only one sound; that is truth absolute. You should follow the twin ideals, "Speak the truth and do righteous deeds." God is changeless Truth but no one understands this. You can do so only when you follow the righteous path of morality and integrity.*

*Man has become a slave to money. He may forget God but will never forget money. You provide yourself with an air conditioner, a good bed, fans and other accessories with a view to having a comfortable sleep. But you do not get sleep. Why? You should have mental peace to sleep well. Your body, mind, chittha (will power) and Ahamkaara (egotism) being the Inner Instruments must all be oriented towards peace as well as the external limbs and sense organs. This can be achieved only by developing Divine Love, which is selfless love and which always gives and never takes, while worldly love is keen on getting and then forgetting.*

## Harming a fellow being is harming the Divine

Divine Love has no equal. It stands supreme. You pray to God for trivial worldly things. You should ask for something that you do not have. You are not having selfless love; hence you should only ask for love which the Divine has in plenty. God is the embodiment of bliss. Pray for love, peace and bliss. You should be able to distinguish between earthly happiness and divine bliss. Today, people pray for many trifles. God knows what is good for the devotee and gives it. He is a witness to all the thoughts, words and actions. Therefore, surrender wholeheartedly without any reservation whatsoever to God, and lead an ideal life. You are all embodiments of the Divine. So you should love all and never hurt anyone. If you harm anyone, you are harming the Divine.

St. John used to consider all as his brothers. But, on one occasion he punished one brother, Jesus appeared in his dream and questioned him, "Do you think you are hurting that man? No, you are hurting Me." You should understand this truth that any harm done to a fellow-being is harming the Divine. You should cultivate the spirit of Oneness.

Bhajan, meditation, etc., are only exercises for purifying the mind. "Chitthasya Shuddhaye Karmane". Develop love which is your life-breath. When a tree is full of green leaves, branches and fruits, you are attracted by it. When it becomes dry, you destroy it because there is no life in it. A person without love is akin to a dead tree only.

Love is as vital for a human as fire is vital for a lump of coal to sparkle. You should get rid of weakness by concentrating on Divine Love, as Divine Grace confers the greatest strength. All other things may come and go but Divine Grace is ever flowing. Whatever you *may or may not be able to do, develop Divine Love. God is the director and all humans are mere actors. Be good performers in God's play. Only to train you for this role, this Youth Conference has been convened. In the midst of the world replete with fear, distrust and mutual recrimination, you have to prove yourself to be the messengers of the Divine and the embodiments of love, peace and truth. Declare your reality as Divine to the world at large and make them realize the Divinity in everyone.*

*Embodiments of love! You young men and women should know what is truth, what is love and what is God and what relationship is there between mind and world. Youth go abroad in quest of money. You are not satisfied with what you can earn here and out of greed you go for earning more. You should have your hands in society and your head in the forest. This is a real rest. Men spend their entire life with attachment to money to such an extent that even while on their death bed they cannot think of God. In this conference, you have been told about fear of sin and morality in society. You have to carry these ideals with you and practise them.*

### God is the hero, rest are Zeros

*You must radiate human values and ensure unity in thought, word and deed. At present there is chaos and mutual animosity amongst various people. You have to spread the message of unity, purity and divinity.*

*Vivekaananda said: "Give me ten men who are pure and perfect. I can change the whole world." But I say, "I can bring about transformation even with one truly perfect human being." You should have divine as the base number one. Any number of zeros placed alongside the figure of one will carry value; value increases many fold with its additional zeros. But, without the number one, if you put zeros, they carry no value at all. The Divine is ONE. Sun, moon, earth, etc., are all mere zeros. They get value only because of the primary number ONE, which represents the Divine. So God is the hero and the rest are all zeros! Have full faith in God and surrender to God. Do service with a spirit of dedication as an offering to God. Spread the message of the glory of God in every village by chanting the name of God. Then the atmosphere and climate of the world will change for the better and become sacred.*

Discourse during the World Youth Conference
on July 17, 1997 in Sai Kuluanth Mandap.

# FOUR CHILD DEVELOPMENT DUTIES

T he American population is presently moving from married couples raising children to *single* parents. The experts are telling us that *stress* is one of the major causes.

Our lifestyle is fast-paced, noisy, polluted and stimulating. Is it any wonder that we are stressful? There is very little down-time. I don't believe that our nervous systems were designed to handle the amount of "in-coming mail", the stimuli, that bombard us, and that we allow each day. All this activity, along with financial pressure to maintain a lifestyle that demands many times for both parents to be working, can create stress for both husbands and wives.

In our complex society, the job of raising children is definitely a two-parent job. Even with two parents attending the children, the job is overwhelming. We actually need a word that is stronger than **STRESS**, to express adequately our intense lifestyle.

In corporate America there is a new term emerging called "Daddy Stress". Corporations are familiar with the role of working woman; they accept her dual role as both employee and mother. Not true for the father. Corporations give women time to leave work if a child is sick, to have flexible work hours and/or extended leave for child-birth. Some companies even provide day-care facilities.

The role of the family man is also changing to accommodate their working wives. Fathers are assuming more childcare responsibilities as well, and dads just want more "hands on" time with their children. Unfortunately, the corporations have different priorities. Men are expected to stay late, travel anywhere, anytime, and family life should not hinder their obligation to the company in any way. Because of this men are having what is called "daddy stress."

Example: father is invited to attend his daughter's class for one hour, when his employer at the last minute wants him to go to a meeting. The company is not sympathetic to his daddy role and his heart is torn because he wants to be with his child instead of attending the meeting. If he stays at work, his daughter's heart is crushed, but he can't risk losing his job.

So take a moment to review our householder activities to understand the gigantic assignment, and see if we can find a way to eliminate some of our stress. Parents have four categories of child development duties: physical, intellectual, emotional and spiritual.

## THE PHYSICAL DEVELOPMENT

The household must be maintained.. This includes all the physical repairs, cleaning, purchasing and usage of supplies. Take a moment and look around your house. You will see countless items that you purchased and have to maintain. Each item needs to be cleaned and repaired. We are truly possessed by our possessions.

Sai Baba says, *"Do all household work as acts of worship for Him; that is more fruitful than hours of meditation, hours gained by entrusting this precious work to paid helpers."* SSS #7 pg. 146

Shopping can be a stressful time consumer. We travel to purchase an item, and most of the time to save money you must do a price comparison. Sometimes you get the item home and it's broken or doesn't fit. The whole scenario is reenacted. The question I ask myself every time I go to purchase an item is, can I live without this?

Sai Baba says, *"Money has to be given its own place of importance. It has to be used in the best way possible. Because you do not make the best use of any given thing, you cannot understand what it is there for. You should, for instance use the power of intelligence to avoid the misuse of money."*

Feeding the family is not a choice, it is a necessity, and a huge time consuming task. Marketing, storing, cleaning, cooking and clean-up can eat up our day. Many families, are frequent flyers at the "Fast Food" restaurants, as well as junk food addicts. This is certainly costly in terms of money and health. Can we find creative ways of eating simple healthy foods with less time for preparation?

Sai Baba says, *"Food plays a major role in the upkeep of health. Care should be taken to see that the food consumed does not have much fat content, for the fats consumed in large quantity are detrimental not only to one's physical health but also affect mental health, whereby man loses human values."* International Symposium on cardiovascular diseases January 21, 1994

Parents are snagged into the peer pressure scene of keeping up with the "Jones". If the neighbors or friends take their children to sport camps, music, karate and dance class, over-night with friends, out for pizza, or birthday celebrations, then our children expect the same. This peer pressure extends to name brand clothes, toys, video games, sports equipment etc., etc. Parents feel guilty if they cannot provide for their children as their friends do. Unfortunately, the inner character is seldom emphasized, only the outer wrapping, or should I say "trappings."

Sai says, *"Man is never satisfied. He is greedy for more and more wealth. What man has to earn is divine grace. No matter what he earns, he cannot take a single pie with him when he leaves the body."* SS May 99 pg. 135

Sai Baba says, *"Children must learn thrift and the proper use of money. When children learn how to use money with care and without waste, the future will be bright."* SSS #7 pg. 146

There seems to be a universal epidemic of material gain; corporations report record sales. When you stop and examine all the time spent in these endeavours, plus the time and pressures of  earning the income to pay for these items, is there any doubt that our lifestyle is "purchase driven"? This factor is contributing to 'big time' STRESS in our family life, because we are working more and more hours to purchase what we consider to be essential for living. The question we must ask: "What do we really need versus what the advertising industry tells us we need?"

Parents are depleted in time, money and energy. They tell me that there is no time for their family or themselves. They are just plain tired. Time management is not just a term for the office. Your home life needs to be evaluated in terms of reducing your workload. If you have less food preparation, less items to purchase and maintain, less individual activities for your children and self, you might find more time for relaxation and family togetherness. Cut out the excess, and have less stress!

Sai Baba says, *"Do not waste time; time is God; time waste is life waste."* SS April 1999 pg. 99

Home management is an enormous task which addresses the physical needs of a family. The intellectual, emotional, and spiritual needs of rearing children are equally as time consuming.

## INTELLECTUAL DEVELOPMENT

Education develops the intellect. From the onset of early childhood development, parents are teaching their child the knowledge that is necessary to function in society. Swami tells us that parents are the child's first teachers. They teach the children the basic knowledge needed for living in society, as well as language, writing, reading, math, and manners.

Swami says, *"Education is for life, not for money."* SS May '99 pg. 134

Even though your child enters the educational system, there are still hours of follow-up homework, and school activities. The education of a child spans from conception through university. This is usually a 22-year investment, which extends with each additional child. Before you decide to have children be sure that you are aware of the formidable commitment and responsibility.

Sai Baba says, *"It is utterly selfish to come to Prasanthi Nilayam to do service activity. You may come after retirement for service at Prasanthi Nilayam. You have your own duties to your children, for their education and career."* SS April 1999 pg. 99

## EMOTIONAL DEVELOPMENT

Small children love to drag around a small blanket for security. Loving feelings are a security blanket that we wrap around our children's bodies, minds, and hearts with care. Emotions are energy waves, broadcasting like radio waves, that a child immediately registers and absorbs. If you are fearful, anxious, nervous, negative, angry, etc., they know it! If you are happy, joyful, playful, positive, peaceful, confident, etc., they know it! They feel what you transmit. Is your own emotional stability important to your child? You bet it is.

You can tell me that you love me a thousand times, but if I don't feel it, I don't believe it. Every communication happens on many levels. Your words may carry a meaning similar to or completely different from the feeling with which it is said. The very first message of "I'm okay, you're okay" is transmitted by the parents. Your response to your child tells them who they are? This is developing their self-esteem. A child needs to know that they are loved and accepted, that they have a home that is a secure place for them to discover and explore their reality.

A good relationship between husband and wife is a stabilizing influence for their children. A child feels deeply the nature of their parents' union and is profoundly affected positively or negatively by this primary example of relationship. Quarrels, back-biting, fighting, dishonesty, withholding or withdrawing from each other threaten the child's sense of security and well-being. Children feel troubled and insecure, instead they need to experience their parents' loving one another honestly.

Swami says, *"Love is the undercurrent of human life. Man will be able to manifest his innate divinity only when he develops love within."* SS May 1999 pg. 113

The complexity of parenting is awesome, because we have such a profound effect on our child. And to think it was just a few years ago, in the 1960's, that the media informed us that the job of motherhood can easily be left in the hands of unskilled women. This inferred that the task of rearing children is so insignificant that anyone can raise a child. Today, the same notion is presenting itself in the developing nations around the world.

I read an article from a National Indian Newspaper, date January 16, 1999, called "Roles of a Life-Time." I quote,

"From being mere housewives, holding ladles and changing nappies, women have emerged from the cocoon of traditions to assert their independence in a rapidly changing technology-dominated world......women are becoming aware of their skills and potentials beyond the realms of home and family. 'A women's place is in the home'. This adage, has no place today as women scale great heights in diverse fields, carving a niche for themselves in a hitherto male dominated corporate world."

Women are still being presented erroneous facts, "that only in the workplace can their full potential be realized". To mould the character of a child takes more knowledge, skill, character, and spirituality than any position in business.

Sai Baba tells us, *"Due to the effect of Kali Age, people consider their mothers as mere cooks in the kitchen. Not only that, they have been degraded to the level of servants. This is the misfortune that has befallen on man today. Women can study, undertake jobs, but they should not neglect their household duties. If both husband and wife go to office, who will look after the household responsibilities? If women go to schools to teach others' children who will teach their own children? Mothers are responsible for the well-being of their children."* Ladies'Day Discourse 11\19\98

**TELEVISION STRESS**

Television adds to the stress load of parenting today. The households of my parents' generation were dominated by parental influence, and the task of raising children was *much easier.* Today, our children are influenced by strangers, television, movies internet etc., who may or may not share our values.

In the media circus of movies and television, there is no protection or sacredness, no guardian of morality for our children's formidable years. Their senses are laid bare to every conceivable horror, evil, and violent behaviour which most adults cannot emotionally evaluate. I have heard Swami say that television is the unraveling of morality in the world.

Sai says, *"The whole world is suffering from the consequences of Television. The world is racked by disorder, discord and frustration."* SS January 15, 1996

Parents moulding the character of their children with Sai values must spend as much time and effort *remoulding* the unwanted morality that is creeping in through outside influence. In many homes, after school hours are spent helping children understand and cope with the negative experiences that they had at school that day......homework being the least of it. For example, I was told a story about Jane, a 12 year old girl. There were 4 girls in Jane's class who wrote a scandalous letter about her. A mother told me, "The letter was filled with so much trash that I cannot even repeat what was said about poor Jane." The letter that ruined this young girl's reputation was then e-mailed to 40 classmates! Only in this age of multi-media could something like this occur.

Swami says, *"Slip while walking, the injury can be repaired, but slip while talking, the injury is irreparable."* Sixteen Spiritual Summers pg. 106

The principal from the school made the 4 girls apologize to Jane; but how can you change, erase or retract this horrible image of a young girl from the minds of 40 classmates? The young girl's reputation, as well as her self-esteem, were injured.

Sai Baba says, *"Youth today have lost confidence in themselves. They are affected by criticism levelled against them. They should see that if the criticism is justified, they should correct themselves. If it is not justified, they should ignore it. If you are criticized for a fault that is not in you,*

41

*you can ignore it even if the whole world joins in the criticism."* SS January 15, 1996

## SPIRITUAL DEVELOPMENT

Spirituality is not a separate theme but is woven with a fine gold thread into the fabric of the physical, mental and emotional needs of a child.

Sai Baba teaches us, *"The primary responsibility of a parent is to mould the character of their child."*

Character is taught continuously from day to day and year to year. It is the fibre of their personality. Our character determines, who and what type of person we are. We teach by our example, which means we also need to change our own behaviour. All of us know how long it takes to change an unwanted behaviour. Don't allow an unwanted behaviour to root in your child because he/she will eventually need to uproot it. If they carry the diseased character trait out of your home it will be transplanted into their home.

Sai says, *"Discipline must start from the early years."* *SS July 1996 pg. 175*

Not only must we be an example of Sai Baba's teachings but we need to instill these loving values in our children. Words, when they are not enforced by the ropes of discipline, fall away. Our children need love to build character but love that is tough, tough enough to allow them to suffer the consequences of their actions. To walk the fine line of law and love is an unequalled balancing act. Our Beloved Sai is a Master.

Spiritual education will take most of your time, since you are battling many external forces that are suffocating your voice of decency, which seems to be heard by the children as an almost silent whisper. Parents are troubled by the lack of influence they have over their child's behaviour. They worry countless hours, and when the children reach puberty, their arms are never long enough to hold them within the boundaries that have at a younger age, been visual. Parents, often don't know what is happening in the life of their teenage or college age child.

Sai says, *"The situation in the outside world is appalling. Even tenth standard students are taking to drink and drugs. The parents are not restraining them. Nor are they setting a good example. When the parents exchange words, the children exchange blows. The parents give a free rein to the children instead of controlling them."* SS May 1996 pg. 119

We are assisting the development of our childrens' conscience, which is the most important asset you can encourage to protect them in life. The conscience is the lifeline between the child and you when they are not beside you. They must hear your voice speaking inside, guiding them as to what is right and wrong.

After evaluating the four categories of parental responsibilities in this chapter, the logical answer is to lessen the physical needs of your family. It is the only area you can safely reduce because emotional security, education and spiritual development are crucially important and usually need greater attention. The question is: How can you manage your food, money, time and energy more efficiently? If you spend less money by curtailing your shopping, entertainment and individual activities it will give you more time and perhaps a less stressful life. Moms and dads, take time to do this simple exercise. It will benefit the entire family.

Sai Baba says, *"There are four components in the term ceiling on desires. They are, respectively, a curb on excessive talk, a curb on excessive desires and expenditure, control of consumption of food, and a check on waste of energy. Man needs some essential commodities for his sustenance, and he should not aspire for more. We can learn a lesson in this respect from Nature. Only if air is available in sufficient quantity will it be comfortable and good. If it is excessive and there is a gale, you will feel uncomfortable. When you are thirsty, you can consume only a limited quantity of water. You can't consume the entire water of the Ganges! We take only as much as is needed for the sustenance of the body.*

*So we should not waste food, money, time, and energy. Even in purchase of garlands, you need not waste money. What God wants is the flower of your heart that is filled with humility and devotion."* SS April 1983 pgs. 84-85

# CHAPTER 5
# BIG QUESTION! CAREER OR STAY AT HOME?

*"The Feminine Principle is spoken of as the illusion imposed on Himself by the Lord, as the Energy with which He equipped Himself out of His own will. This is why Woman is considered to be an embodiment of the Supreme Shakti. She is the faithful companion of man, his fortune; since she is the concretization of the Will of the Lord, she is Mystery, Wonder, the representative of the protective Principle. She is the queen of man's home, his beneficence, the illumination of his house. Women are in no way inferior (to men) for they are the repositories of the divine Force."*

Sai Baba *Dharma Vahini* Ch.4

The role of women changed dramatically during this century. In the 1940's, when husbands went to war, a significant population of women left their home to work in the defence factories. This event, more than any other, introduced a greater number of women to the workplace. "Rosie The Rivetor" became the poster girl for women who heard the call to help our country at war. When industry shifted to a peacetime economy many of the women remained in the workforce. Because most were uneducated, they held positions in the labour taskforce.

45

In 1963, Betty Friedan in her book, The Feminine Mystique, raised the issue of gender inequality. That same year Congress passed the Equal Pay Act, which made it illegal to use gender as a rational for pay discrimination. At that time for comparable work, women earned an average of .58 cents for every dollar earned by a man. Women were fighting for their "Equal Rights."

Swami says, *"Unfair things happen in the world with respect to women. That is why we decided to celebrate not only 19 November but the 19th of every month as Women's Day."* Discourse April 19, 1998

In 1972 Gloria Steinem published a feminist magazine. The first issue sold out its run of 300,000 copies in eight days. That same year the anti-feminist movement emerged as activist Phyllis Schlafly opposed the Equal Rights Amendment.

The 60's and 70's were turbulent years, that had women not only seeking their identity, but their self-worth. Women wanted recognition of their value in our society. They wanted equal participation in the worldly affairs of men. Could women equally compete in the job market? This became the focus of the feminist movement.

One answer surfaced, forty years later, in the February 1999 Issue of USA Today, when Gloria Steinem said, "The majority of the country now believes that women can do what men can do. But we haven't begun to realize that men can do what women can do."

Sai says, *"Men say a man is known by his job, as though only males can do jobs. This is a misnomer. Women are now doing all work equal to men. In fact, women work more sincerely and with more dedication. Recently, a director of the Indian Telephone Industries came to see Swami. Swami questioned him about the percentage of women employed in the industry. He said 99 percent of those employed there were women; he added that women performed ten times better than men. Women do not stop or step out until the allotted work is completed. They have a better work ethic than men."* Discourse April 19, 1998

Unfortunately, Equal Rights became synonymous with "identical" in the mind of many women. In an effort to be like men, women began to adopt male behaviour, including their negative habits of smoking, drinking, and swearing. Socializing in the workplace became acceptable behaviour. This desire to be the "same" has just added confusion to woman's search for her identity.

In 1960 the illusion of sexual freedom accompanied the introduction of the birth-control pill. It was not available however for the poor population, because it took money and education to use this pill. Without prevention, sexual freedom produced the consequences of unwanted pregnancy. Our youth received the wrong message: that promiscuous behaviour is acceptable. In 1997, 32.4% of births came from unmarried mothers, and the percentage of births to teenagers to us 12.8%. Monthly Vital Statistics Report, Vol 46, No. 1 Supplement 2

Swami said to the boy students. *"You give women cigarettes. You give them pants. Do you wear Sari's? Can you have children? No, you are not equal. Equality only at the ATMIC Level."*

The Feminist message of the 1960's, brought about the loss of male and female identity in the home. There were three such messages:

1. If there is a child in the room, it makes no difference whether a mother or father is present with the child. Gender is inconsequential.

2. No title of mother or father, only, *parent* is important; as long as there is one.

3. Marriage is not important as long as there is a relationship in the home.

Much of my own confusion over the role of a woman has been clarified by our Beloved Swami, but I will never forget the turmoil of women seeking to establish their place and contribution in society during those years. The emphasis of women in the sixty's and seventy's was equality with men, on their turf, outside the home. The only way women could get recognition was in the workplace, politics, sports and entertainment; all these activities were outside the home.

Who was going to record their achievements inside the home? Men were doing the evaluating, and salaries weren't paid for raising children. Men knew little about work inside the home so how could a woman's worth be assessed, unless women challenged men in their own arena?

So women became educated and entered the work force. A recent study from the Census Bureau says that in 1998, for the first time, younger women (ages 25-29) pass men in high school graduation, 88.9% to 85.8%, and in college degrees, 29.3% to 26.3%.

Sai Baba says, *"It is not my view that women should not get educated. They should have education. You may also take up jobs. But you should live up to the obligations and glory of womanhood."* SS December 1966 pg. 333

The women who stayed at home were not recognized as having any worth during these struggling and changing years. Being a **"stay-at-home-mom"** had little self esteem.

Sai says, *"People generally speak of women as the weaker sex. Bharatiyas recognize that women cannot be considered weak. The woman in charge of the home plays the main role in bringing good name and fame to the household. Similarly, women play a major role in upholding the prestige of the state, the country and even the world."* Discourse Kodaikanal Ladies' Day April 19, 1998

Forty years have passed and society still fails to recognize the importance of a mother's presence in the home. It is crucial to the development of a child's character. Still most of the studies "say" kids aren't harmed by having working mothers. Humorously, I might add, a recent study placed a value of $170,000 per annum on the myriad tasks performed by a mother who stays at home. The conclusion is that stay-at-home moms, also have monetary value.

The feminist movement confused my role as a woman. Was it more important for me to contribute to society through additional education and working outside the home? Was staying at home a job that any servant could fulfill? The job of wife and mother often included unending and thankless tasks, the daily monotony of cleaning, cooking and child rearing. Nothing in my daily routine was permanent, and it was difficult to see any work you accomplished at the end of the day. The food was eaten, the house messed-up, the clothes dirty etc. What was contributed, physically, mentally, emotionally, and spiritually was not visible and easily forgotten. The value of being a wife and mother was buried under women's drive to become educated and marketable.

For me, only dear Swami affirmed and reassured me of the importance of mothers staying at home. He was the one that raised my consciousness and self-esteem. He brought solace and joy into my heart by confirming that the job of keeping a home and raising children was contributing to society in an important manner.

Sai says, *"Help as much as you can, as efficiently as you can, as silently as you can, as lovingly as you can; leave the rest to God, who gave you a chance to serve."* Vision of Sai I, pg. 126

When a career women becomes a mother, it is very difficult for her to quit her profession. She muses, "Why doesn't the husband stay home? Why should I be the one to sacrifice my career?"

Sai says, *"Men do not have the same spirit of sacrifice as women. If any problem arises, men come forward with initial enthusiasm, but it is only women who resolutely fight until success is achieved."* SS November 19, 1995

Women sacrifice excitement, mental challenge, interaction with peers, luncheon dates, and sometimes travel to change diapers and feed and comfort. This lure of the adult world when competing with the demands of a child is the challenge of conscience every loving mother confronts. A stay-at-home mom must take a conscious leap from self interest to selflessness.

Sai says, *"In this phenomenal world, whatever pleasures and satisfactions one may derive elsewhere, if there is no joy at home, it becomes a veritable hell. The home is heaven itself. It is the duty of women to maintain it as such."* SS December 1996 pg. 334

In America, 76 percent of mothers are working outside the home; 10 million children under the age of 5 have employed mothers. (Census Bureau, latest available figures 1999) Stay-at-home moms are the exception today. Our children are suffering because their mothers are working. I have seen little children in day-care centers who are sick. They were lying alone on the floor. How can a limited day-care staff adequately mother more than a few of the many toddlers in their facility?

Swami tells us, *"The child should grow with the mother for the first 5 years of life. Many children do not know what the love of the mother is like. The mother should not hand over her responsibility during these years to some one else and be called simply 'Mummy' as if she is some doll with which the child likes to play. Now, the children of rich and "educated" parents are severely handicapped. They are deprived of the care and love of the parents. They are handed over to the care of servants and ayahs and they grow up in their company and learn their vocabulary and habits and styles of thought. This is very undesirable."* Divine Discourse Whitefield May 5, 1962

Regrettably, some mothers are forced to work due to economic hardship, and the numbers are increasing. For the family however that can manage to live with less so that their child can have more of mom, the benefits can be enormous. There is simply no substitute for a mother's love in the development of a child, especially during those early critical years.

I repeat, if there is any way possible for you and your spouse to live with less so that your child can have more of mom, it is the ideal. This step will take a great deal of sacrifice and discrimination, but your child will benefit beyond what was once believed.

Swami says, *"If women go out for jobs who will take care of the homes? If husband and wife go to offices, who will look after the children? Earning money may solve some problems but how will it resolve domestic problems? Truly speaking, working women do not enjoy much happiness."* SS December 1996 pg. 333

Today, science has given us more understanding and proof of brain development in a child from birth to 10 years. Only now are we learning the importance of a mother being with her child.

A special report from Time Magazine called **FERTILE MINDS**, headlines:

**"FROM BIRTH, A BABY'S BRAIN CELLS PROLIFERATE WILDLY, MAKING CONNECTIONS THAT MAY SHAPE A LIFETIME OF EXPERIENCE. THE FIRST THREE YEARS ARE CRITICAL."**

"Researchers at Baylor College of Medicine, have found that children who don't play much or are rarely touched develop brains 20% to 30% smaller than normal for their age.

The new insights into brain development are more than just interesting science. They have profound implications for parents and policy makers. In an age when mothers and fathers are increasingly pressed for time and may already be feeling guilty about how many hours they spend away from their children the results coming out of the labs are likely to increase concerns about leaving very young children in the care of others. For the data underscore the importance of hands-on parenting, of finding the time to cuddle a baby, talk with a toddler and provide infants with stimulating experiences. There is a time-scale to brain development, and the most important year is the first, notes Frank Newman, president of the Education Commission of the States." Time February 3, 1997 Vol.149 No.5

Sai Baba says, *"There is no diviner or purer feeling than maternal love. The mother and the motherland are greater than heaven itself."* SS December 1992 pg. 283

**Dr. Susan Johnson reports:**

"Joseph Chilton Pearce in his book, Evolution's End, sees a child's potential as a seed that needs to be nurtured and nourished in order to grow properly. If the environment doesn't provide the necessary nurturing (and protections from over-stimulation), then certain potentials and abilities cannot be realized. The infant is born with 10 billion nerve cells or neurons and spends the first three years of life adding billions of glial cells to support and nourish these neurons (Everett 1992). These neurons are then capable of forming thousands of interconnections with each other via spider-like projections called dendrites and longer projections called axons that extend to other regions of the brain.

It is important to realize that a six-year-old's brain is 2\3 the size of an adult's though it has 5 - 7 times more connections between neurons than does the brain of an 18 month old child or an adult (Pearce 1992). The brain of a 6 - 7 year old appears to have a tremendous capacity for making thousands and thousands of dendrite connections among neurons. This potential for development ends around age 10 - 11, when the child loses 80% of these neural connections (Pearce 1992, Buzzell 1998). It appears that what we don't develop or use, we lose as a capacity. An enzyme is released within the brain and literally dissolves all poorly myelinated pathways.

"These myelinated pathways are the key to learning windows. By age 4, both the core (action) and limbic (feeling) brains are 80% myelinated. After age 6 - 7, the brain's attention is shifted to the neocortex (thought brain) with myelination beginning first on the right side or hemisphere and later joined by the left hemisphere.

"The left hemisphere dominates when a child reads, writes and speaks. It specializes in analytical and sequential thinking and step - by - step logical reasoning. It analyzes the sound and meaning of language (e.g., phonic skills of matching sound to letters of the alphabet). It manages fine muscle skills and is concerned with order, routine and details. The ability to comprehend science, religion, maths (especially geometry) and philosophy relies on abstract thinking characteristic of the left hemisphere." (Healy 1990)

Pearce 1992, shows that during a child's development, there are a series of time periods, or " learning windows," in which a child can best learn or refine a particular ability, such as speech. After this time period, it becomes more difficult. By one year the child has established its ability to understand words. By 2 years, the child's vocabulary will be determined by how many different words he hears. The ability to think, learn or not learn is developed by the age of 3.

"To stimulate more language comprehension, you need to talk a lot with your child, especially during this window. Or to help the child be more coordinated or active later in life, you should encourage him or her to run and play games, especially during the window to develop gross muscle coordination. To make your child multilingual, you could teach him or her a new language during the language window." Learning Windows and the Child's Brain by Amy Markezich, Stanford University

"Indeed, parents are the child first and most important teachers. Among other things, they appear to help babies learn by adopting the rhythmic, high-pitched speaking style known as Parentese. When speaking to babies, Stanford University psychologist Anne Fernald has found, mothers and fathers from many cultures change their speech patterns in the same peculiar ways. "They put their faces very close to the child," she reports. They use shorter utterances, and they speak in an unusually melodious fashion." The heart rate of infants increases while listening to Parentese, even Parentese delivered in a foreign language. Moreover, Fernald says, Parentese appears to hasten the process of connecting words to the objects they denote. FERTILE MIND Time February 3, 1997 VOL. 149 NO.5

"Psychiatrists and educators have long recognized the value of early experience, but their observations have until now been largely anecdotal. 'What's so exciting', says Matthew Melmed, executive director of Zero to Three, a nonprofit organization devoted to highlighting the importance of the first three years of life, 'is that modern neuroscience is providing the hard, quantifiable evidence that was missing earlier. Because you can see the results under a microscope or in a PET scan', he observes, 'it's become that much more convincing." *FERTILE MINDS* Time February 3, 1997 VOL. 149 NO. 5

Sai Baba says, *"Women are endowed with exceptional strength. Even in the spiritual field women display their boundless capacity. It is in her role as mother that there is the highest expression of a woman's strength. The mother is the first teacher of speech, the first steps in movement and many other primary lessons in behaviour."* SS June 1996 pg. 157

Science is now providing the proof that a stay-at-home mom determines the capacity of their child's learning abilities. Could it be that finally society will value the stay-at-home mom? How long has it been that women have toiled in the field to raise their children with little praise or approval? How sweet it is to finally know that the job we do on a day-to-day treadmill with the kids is actually having a definitive influence, and one far beyond our wildest expectations.

We get so involved in the daily routine of being a mother, that we easily loose sight of the incredible journey of giving birth to a child, bringing an infant to his feet, to his first day at school and to his College Graduation. Many events take place between these benchmarks in our child's life that we influence in a positive or negative manner. The challenge that lies before us is remarkable.

Swami tells us, *"For lakhs of students and children who go to school, the mother is the first teacher. From the moment of birth, for every one the mother is the preceptor. If such a teacher leaves her home to teach other children, who will teach her children?"* SS December 1996 pg. 334

After centuries of female suppression, now is the time for women to shine, every bit as bright as the male energy. The genders are gloriously different, not equal in characteristics, but equal in their ability and necessity to contribute. We need to stand tall, and realize that the male and female energy each have a place in the heart of God. Each has special gifts to offer. Why can't we enhance the unique characteristics of the male and female energy within each other, our families and the world? This is the design of the Creator.

In conclusion, women have not been fully recognized for their talents, strengths, and virtues. They have fought a heroic fight for their equal rights. Whether a woman is in the workplace or in the home, she is a magnificent instrument. The world in general has been reluctant to acclaim her, but not our beloved Sai Baba. He has taught me the glory of being a woman. He has not only taught me that my nature is Divine, but who I am, as The Divine Woman!

*"If only women were given their due recognition and encouragement, they would shine with brilliance in all fields and would serve the house, the country and the entire world gloriously, contributing to the welfare of all humanity."* Sai Baba Discourse April 19, 1998

# WOMEN, THE FOUNTAIN OF HUMAN VALUES

## DIVINE DISCOURSE

*"Life in this phenomenal world is impermanent.*
*Whatever is perceived is bound to pass away*
*some time or other.*
*Youth and wealth are transient.*
*Wife and children will pass away.*
*Only Truth and Fame endure."*

### Mother's Influence

*Embodiments of Love!* Human beings are considered to be the epitome of creation in this world which is teaming with millions of beings. In this vast creation, women occupy a very superior position. There are several instances which prove that women are really superior.

Was it not because of boons granted to Kausalya that the Divine took birth in her womb as Rama? Lava and Kusa (sons of Rama and Sita) became great as they were lovingly nurtured by their mother, Sita. Again, Shivaji (a famous Indian emperor) became valorous and great because of the loving care of his mother. Gandhi gained fame and a good reputation because of the care and encouragement that he received from his mother, Putalibai. All people — great sages, warriors, various heroes, virtuous person and even the wicked —

are born of the womb of the mother. Women are the embodiment of Prakrithi Devi (the feminine principle of creation).

The Gayatri Mantra is said to be the basis of the Vedas. Gayatri is the feminine aspect. The Vedas are respected as "Mother Veda". Throughout the past, women have been praised and respected. Women occupy an important place in Vedic prayers, Vedic tradition and Vedic worship. From this, we can say that women have an exalted position.

In the Vedic mode of worship, the four Vedas have been named: Sathyavathi, Angavathi, Anyavathi and Nidanavathi (a name ending in vathi indicates that it is feminine).

The name of Satyavathi signifies that God pervades the whole universe. God is not different from nature. Divinity is the embodiment of the Supreme, the Primal Person, Nature and Creation. Just as butter is present in every drop of milk, God is present in every atom of creation.

Angavathi means that the five elements are present throughout nature — earth, water, fire, air, ether. Of these five elements, each one is more subtle than the other. The Vedas proclaim that these five elements are the forms of God. For that reason, this Veda is known as Angavathi.

The third name is Anyavathi which signifies that certain symbols stand for certain manifestations of God. For instance, Shiva is described as one who holds the trident, and is the "three-eyed one". Vishnu holds the conch, the discus, the mace and the lotus in his hands. Rama is the one who holds the bow. Anyavathi worship suggests that each form of God has certain specific symbols.

Then comes Nidanavathi. Nidanavathi lays down nine different paths one can take to reach God.

## The Nine Steps

The Vedas declare that there are nine steps in the devotional pilgrimage toward God:

* Listening to the glories of God and His handiwork (Shravanam).

* Singing about the Lord and chanting His name (Kirtanam).

* Contemplating on the Lord and revelling in His beauty, majesty and compassion (Smaranam).

* Worshiping the Lord by concentrating on honouring His feet or footprints (Padasevanam).

* A regular pattern of systematic worship (Archanam).

* Reverence toward the Lord, seeing Him in all life and creation (Vandanam).

* Becoming a devoted servant of the Lord by serving all without a feeling of inferiority or superiority (Dasyam).

* Friendship with the Lord, a stage when the seeker feels so close to the Lord that one has the feeling that one is a confidant, companion and sharer of God's power, glory, triumphs and achievements (Sakhyam).

* Total surrender to the Divine Will of the Lord (Atma Nivedanam).

## When Women Are Respected

The feminine aspect of these names — Satyavathi, Angavathi, Anyavati and Nidanavathi are attributed to the Vedas. Names are different, but Divinity is One. Therefore, we should not consider the feminine principle as something insignificant. From time immemorial, the feminine principle has been worshipped in different forms. The Vedas declare that wherever women are respected and given their rightful place, there, Divinity is present with all the facets of its glory. Unfortunately today, respecting women is considered disgraceful and insignificant — something which is not proper.

*The women should be respected as the Goddess of Prosperity in the home (Grihalakshmi). She is the companion of her husband in the fulfillment of the duties and rights of wedded life, and she is a partner in the pilgrimage toward God and Self-Realization (Dharmapatni). The woman is considered to be half the body of her husband (Ardhangi).*

*Nowadays, people feel proud when they win titles for their outstanding contributions in the fields of art, science and public life. These titles are insignificant. However, women hold titles which are permanent in nature. A house without a woman is like a jungle. So, men have a responsibility to give the respect and honour that women deserve and insure that they do not shed tears. The home where the woman sheds tears is bound to go to ruin.*

*Woman is the embodiment of these eight-fold powers which are known as the primal creative aspects of God (Adisakthi). They are:*

* *The aspect relating to the sound of Brahman or God (Sabda-Brahma-Mayi).*
* *The aspect which relates to moving and nonmoving (Charachara-Mayi).*
* *The aspect of effulgence (Jyothir-Mayi).*
* *The aspect of speech (Vang-Mayi).*
* *The aspect of constant happiness and joy (Nityananda-Mayi).*
* *The aspect of this world and the other world (Paratpara-Mayi).*
* *The aspect of illusion (Maya-Mayi).*
* *The aspect of prosperity (Sree-Mayi).*

*These are the names that signify the powers that are present in women. These aspects or titles are all facets of the Divine that pervade the cosmos.*

## Other Feminine Qualities

Ladies also have the worthy name of woman or sthree. This word "sthree" has three syllables in it — sa, tha, and ra. Sa stands for good, pure or (satwaguna) qualities. This signifies constant thought of God, cultivating nearness to God, and a super-causal state wherein the individual experiences unity with God. Satwic nature is inherent in women.

To some extent, women also have dull, lethargic qualities (thamoguna) represented by the syllable tha. Thamasic qualities do not mean merely eating, drinking and sleeping, which makes one lazy. Thamoguna also denotes sensitivity, humility and a mild temperament. Therefore, a woman initially starts her life with thamoguna, having a very passive, giving nature but being very careful to protect the honour and respect of the family. That is the reason why it is said in Andhra Pradesh, "You judge a house by looking at the housewife". As the homemaker, so the home.

The third syllable, ra, stands for active, passionate qualities, (rajoguna). Here rajoguna does not denote aggressiveness or the fighting quality of a woman. If the situation demands, or if the respect of the family is at stake, women do not hesitate to even sacrifice their lives. Our history is replete with examples of women who have fought and won many a battle to protect their country and their honour. This is the characteristic of rajoguna. To fight for truth and to preserve and protect it even at the cost of one's life, is a sign of rajoguna.

Woman is the embodiment of satwic, rajasic and thamasic gunas or qualities. Today, in spite of having so many wonderful qualities, women are considered to be weak, helpless and lacking in strength, but that is not accurate.

## Secrets of Greatness

It is worth mentioning that whenever women have ruled India or abroad, they have successfully managed the affairs of their countries *without much disturbance or disorder, and have brought peace and harmony to their homelands. There have been emperors, but not one has ruled as well as Queen Victoria. Queen Victoria ruled her kingdom with great courage, justice and care. There were no complaints during her regime. Similarly, in the recent past, Indira Gandhi ruled over India with courage and fortitude. She earned a good name by sacrificing her life for the nation. Indira Gandhi was the only woman in the world who was Prime Minister of a country for twelve long years. Some men have ruled for only a couple of years, and during their short tenure created many problems.*

*Over the years, women have struggled, showing courage and fortitude, and they have dedicated themselves to the welfare of society and prosperity of the motherland. Therefore, the poet, Valmiki (author of the epic, Ramayana), while describing women, has called them, "Embodiments of Sweetness".*

*What is this "sweetness" in the nature of women? Valmiki said that it is the spirit of sacrifice that is sweet. For the sake of the child, the mother is prepared to make any amount of sacrifice. This quality is found only in women. If the child suffers from a critical ailment, the father may say, "It is better if the child dies." But, however fatal may be the disease, the mother makes every effort to save the child. Because of this spirit, women are called "Embodiments of Sacrifice".*

*Men do not have the same spirit of sacrifice as women. If any problem arises, men come forward with initial enthusiasm, but it is only women who resolutely fight until success is achieved.*

*Therefore, Valmiki described women as "Embodiments of Devotion", and he described men as "Embodiments of Knowledge". Men may boast that they are endowed with knowledge, but persons of knowledge and intellect have access only up to the doorstep of the Lord's audience hall. They cannot go beyond it. However, women*

64

*who are the embodiments of devotion, can even enter the Lord's audience hall.*

*Therefore, if we refer to the ancient scriptures and read the lives of great women, we will discover the importance of women in the world. The lessons that Shivaji (a famous ruler of India) learned on the lap of his mother, Jijiabai, made him a brave warrior and a great ruler. Rama could follow the most sacred and righteous path because of the tutelage from his mother, Kausalya.*

*Why was Gandhi called Mahatma (a great soul)? When Gandhi was a child, his mother took a vow that she would eat her first morsel of food only when she heard the song of a cuckoo bird. One day, it was past noon and she had not heard the cuckoo sing, so she did not have her food. Gandhi saw that his mother had not had any food, so he went to the backyard and he started imitating the sound of the bird. After some time, he came inside and requested his mother to partake of her food since the cuckoo had sung. Gandhi's mother realized that it was not the cuckoo, but Gandhi who had imitated the sound of a cuckoo. She caught hold of his ears and shouted, "I am ashamed that a liar is born to me. I feel it a sin to call you my son. Man is the embodiment of truth. He should not resort to falsehood under any circumstances". Gandhi realized that his mother was very upset. The words of his mother pierced his heart like an arrow. From that day on, he never uttered an untruth.*

## Mother — The First Teacher

*It is the mother alone, not the father, who can teach the right lessons to the child and make him or her tread the righteous path. In this modern age, it is the father who teaches his child to utter falsehoods. If the telephone rings when the father is sitting at the dining table and the father is not interested in talking to that person, he asks his child to inform the caller that he, the father, is not at home. So, it is the mother or the father who has taught the child to speak untruth? It is the father who teaches bad habits to the children. When did this practice actually start? It started in the Dwapara Yuga, (the age that preceded our present Kali Yuga, (the age when Krishna lived on earth 5,000 years ago). It all started with Dhritarashtra, the blind king of Hastinapur who had 100 evil sons. Whatever wicked acts that his sons did, the king was simply blind to them and always said that his sons were good. Fathers who do such things are not good fathers. The father who asks his child to seek God is the true father. A teacher who imparts spiritual knowledge is the real teacher.*

*From ancient times, it is only the mothers who have taught their children lessons of truth, righteousness and love. The mother is the first guru to the child. Therefore, Indian culture emphasizes the importance of mother, father, teacher and God. In this order, the mother has the first place.*

*Why does she get the first place? It is the mother who carries the child for nine months in her womb, undergoes all trouble and pain, sacrifices everything for the child, and nurtures the child with love. Therefore, you must honor and revere your mother as God. Once the child is born, it is the father who takes the responsibility to rear the child. So, also, revere your father as God.*

*Why is the mother given the leading place? You all know that we often say "Sita, Rama," but we never say "Rama, Sita". Sita's name comes first and is followed by Rama's name. Similarly, we say "Parvathi, Parameshwar", not "Parameshwar, Parvathi". In the same fashion, we say "Lakshmi, Narayana" and not "Narayana, Lakshmi". Why is it that the name of the woman comes first? Because women are the embodiments of nature and creation. It is only by worshipping nature that one can attain the universal soul (Paramatma). How can one who does not deserve the grace of nature ever attain Paramatma?*

## Grace and Honour

In the Mahabharata War, all the 100 Kauravas (the 100 wicked sons mentioned earlier) had lost their lives. Dhritarashtra and Gandhari, parents of the Kauravas, lamented over the loss of all their children and chided Krishna, saying "O Krishna! Was there not even one among my hundred children who deserved Your Grace? Couldn't you have protected at least one child? What sin have I committed?" Krishna replied, "Gandhari, do not be so hasty to scold me in this manner. When not even a single child of yours ever got the protecting look of his mother, how could you expect God to confer His grace on him? From their very birth, did you ever look at even one of your children with your eyes?"

Gandhari had blindfolded her eyes with a piece of cloth (after her marriage to the blind king Dhritarashtra), and she had never seen any of her children. Therefore, how could such children, who had never had the protective grace of their mother ever aspire to receive God's grace?

In the word "amma", which denotes mother, "a" is the first letter of the alphabet. So, too, mother is the first to be honored. Therefore, she is called "Mother Goddess" (Mathru Devi).

Four important injunctions of the Vedas are:

> Honor the mother as God
>
> Honor the father as God
>
> Honor the teacher as God
>
> Honor the guest as God

Mother gives birth to the child, and she alone has the authority to introduce the father to the child. It is the father who introduces the child to its teacher or guru. Then it is the guru who leads the child to God.

*Nothing except truth and reputation are permanent in this world. You can attain this reputation only when you honor your mother, follow her command, and make yourself deserving to receive her love. Mother's commands should never be disregarded. If you have any doubts at all, then approach her in a pleasing way and get your doubts clarified. But never hurt her feelings. Anyone who hurts the sentiments of one's mother can never be happy in life. One who wounds the feelings of his or her mother today, will receive the same treatment from one's children tomorrow. Therefore, you should first win the love and grace of the mother.*

*Even the Russians are aware of this truth. In Russia, December 8th is observed as Ladies Day. The men give freedom to their women on that day, while the menfolk attend to the kitchen and other chores. Women spend the day in the service of society. They go to the hospitals and serve. The spirit of sacrifice that is expressed while doing service is only found in mothers. When a mother watches somebody shedding tears, her eyes get wet too. Women have so much kindness in them.*

### Run From Bad Company

*However, with the changing times, the hearts of women have become hard. What is the reason for this? Our thoughts are shaped by the company we keep. This world is full of bad elements. As the women of today keep company with such elements, their hearts have turned hard. In modern times, it is very difficult to find the company of good people. It was Einstein who said, "Tell me your company, and I shall tell what you are". Run away from bad companions, keep company with the good and noble, and do meritorious acts day and night. You should never entertain bad company, bad thoughts or bad actions, as the fruits of bad actions will recoil on you sooner or later. Therefore, be careful and vigilant right from the beginning.*

## What Can Parents Do?

*Men should try to understand women, and women should also try to understand men. It is the harmony, peace and mutual love between men and women that brings happiness and peace to the family. People want happiness in the family, but they do not lead exemplary lives. The fault lies with both the husband and the wife. If children have taken the wrong path these days, the parents alone are responsible, as they are not exemplary in their behaviour either.*

*For example, how can you prevent the child from smoking if the father smokes in front of the son? Then he, too, will start smoking by stealing cigarettes from his father's pocket. If the father scolds him for smoking, the modern day child retorts, "Father, when you yourself are smoking, why do you object to my smoking?" Therefore, parents should never behave in a manner that will set a bad example for the children.*

*Sometimes you cry that your children are not listening to your advice, and have gone astray. How can you make them listen to you. Did you listen to the advice of your parents? Whatever you say or do comes back to you. You should have proper control over your children. First of all, have control over yourself. Only when the father is good can he expect his son to be good. Is it possible for him to keep his son at home when he himself roams about as he likes? Nowadays, the father does not try to correct the child, and the child does not listen to the mother. Therefore, 90% of the fathers are like Dhritarashtra; they will accept anything that their children do. This is the reason why the world has come to such a sorry state. If the children take the path of charitable service, faith in God and devotion, the father asks the children, "What is all this madness? Have you also become Sai crazy? Don't participate in service, don't do charity, do not attend devotional singing." Some fathers are like that and some others are like Hiranyakasipu. Some fathers close their ears like*

*Hiranyakasipu did, so that he could not hear his son, Prahlada (an exemplary child who was devoted to God), uttering the name of God. Today, we have only fathers like Dhritarashtra or Hiranyakasipu, while there is a lack of fathers who can guide their children on the right path and set before them some lofty ideals. Some parents preach high ideals, but they cannot correct their own children at home. Who will listen to their sermons? It is easy to speak but difficult to practise.*

*Hence, we should understand the values enshrined in Bharatiya (Indian) culture. These days, children do not show any interest in reading sacred texts. They read all sorts of trash and start on the wrong path in their childhood. If the tender saplings grow straight the tree will also grow straight. If the sapling grows crooked, then the tree will grow crooked. Therefore, love the children, but give them stern correction if they do anything wrong. Timid parents of today fear to establish strict rules for the children, as they may run away from home or end their lives.*

*It is better to live like a swan for two years than to live like a crow for a hundred years. If we want children who will earn a good name in society, and if such children are to be fostered, then, the parents must first correct themselves. When Prahlada defied the commands of his father, King Hiranyakasipu, his mother tried to persuade him in a pleasing manner and said, "My dear son, it is not for you to disregard the commands of your father. Try to obey by any means." Therefore, in all situations, it is the mother who advises the child. So, mothers of today should have pure thoughts and ideals.*

### Noisy Habits

*Whenever women gather in one place, they start gossiping and create noise which sounds like the beat of a drum. You have all been sitting here for a long time, and there has been more noise from the women than the men. It is not that all women create such noise, but for some it is a habit. As we are celebrating Ladies' Day this day, make a resolve that from tomorrow onward, women should limit their talking. Not only here, but in the prayer hall too, it is the women who always talk.*

*Men go on turning and talking as they please. Men set no limits or restraints on themselves. They do not care to ponder over where they should go, why they should go there, nor how they should behave. The women do not know when to talk, what they should say, nor when to maintain silence. Therefore, if men and women correct these habits, then there can be happiness.*

### Mind and Thoughts

*Prahlada told his father, Hiranyakasipu, "You could conquer the whole world, but you have failed to control your own senses. First try to conquer your inner world, then you will conquer the outer world."*

*What is it that is responsible for the well-being of society? Our actions are responsible for the good and bad in the world. Our thoughts are responsible for our actions. Our minds are responsible for our thoughts. Our desires and resolves are responsible for our minds. Therefore, if all the people in the country have the right thoughts, then everything will be all right. So, we should cultivate good, pure ideals and thoughts.*

*One of the ladies who spoke earlier, talked of truth (sathya), righteousness (dharma), peace (shanti), non-violence (ahimsa) and love (prema).*

* *Every word spoken with love is truth. Words emanating from a heart filled with love are truth.*
* *All actions that spring from a loving heart are righteous.*
* *Everything that we contemplate with a heart full of love is peace.*
* *Whatever we do with a heart filled with love can only be non-violent.*

71

✳ *Hence, love is the very foundation of all human values. Without love there is no life. Therefore, everyone must cultivate this quality of love.*

In these times, people become angry for trifling reasons. Anger weakens you. It is said that anger reduces one's life span. It is like a saw which cuts your life asunder. So, you should never have anger or jealousy. It is only thinking of God that will cure you of the diseases of anger and jealousy.

### Nations Are Founded On . . .

In every house and in every corner of the land, spread the message of God as there is no easier path than this.

The feminine principle is something good, virtuous and wonderful. It is only when the women are good that children will be ideal citizens. If the nation is to prosper, then the father and mother must be good. It is very necessary. Countries are in a state of chaos today; therefore, we must see that an atmosphere of peace prevails. For both peace and joy, it is the home that is most important. If there is no joy in the home, how can there be joy in the nation? So, we must experience joy at home first. Then, we should spread joy to the whole state and finally to the whole country. But instead of spreading joy, you are spreading chaos. Disharmony, resulting from fights between husband and wife, is shamelessly demonstrated on the streets. Is it a sign of manliness to exhibit in public the flaws that have developed at home?

Today everybody claims to be educated, but their conduct does not reflect their education. How can persons, who are unable to set right their own homes, ever succeed in setting right the nation? Acquire an education which will help you to reform society and the country.

## Women's Pivotal Role

We always say that the world is full of discord. From where has this discord come? It has come from within us. So, every year on the 19th of November, while celebrating Ladies' Day, these sacred feelings are to be spread all over the world. Not only here, but even while at home women should know how to lead their lives, how to behave with others, and how to tend their children. Even if the husband is wicked, the wife should exercise patience. Ravana — the demon King of Sri Lanka who kidnapped Sita and was defeated by Lord Rama — was a wicked person. But his wife, Mandodari, could live with him because of her forbearance. Mandodari often advised Ravana. She used to say, "Ravana, if the same thing that happened to Sita would have happened to me, how terrible you would feel. Therefore, is it proper for you to behave in this manner? You should not go after the wife of another person. Correct yourself."

## Start Now!

Beginning today, try to correct yourselves. Let men and women consider others' mistakes to be small, however big they may be. Consider your own faults to be big, however small they may be. See the good in others and emulate their good qualities. It is of utmost importance that you see the flaws in yourself and eliminate them. However, today you see the faults of others, not of yourself.

In Telegu there is a proverb that the misguided man always searches for the faults in others, and the dog always searches for the shoes of others. Those who are always on the lookout for the faults in others are like the dogs. Do not become dogs, become Gods. Remember, human life is very sacred and extremely difficult to obtain.

Embodiments of Divine Love! You may have faults, and you should correct them, not repeat them in the future. If you do something wrong to anybody, then you wrong yourself and you will get a bad name. All of you should lead your lives with good *feelings and a good mind. What is a good mind? A mind full of peace, full of love, full of compassion is indeed a good mind.*

## Sai Wants Our Transformation

*Buddha once saw a corpse. Then he saw an old man, and then a sick man, and in an instant Buddha was transformed. Today you may see corpses, old people and sick people, but the experience does not transform you. You have got to change. Where is that truth in you? Where is that righteousness in you?*

*Year after year you hear so many discourses by Swami. How many of you have changed? Where is the transformation in you? The transformation has to come about. Not only here but wherever you go the change has to come about. This should be reflected in your pure feelings and actions. Otherwise, what is the use of spending money to come here?*

*Therefore, on this auspicious occasion of Ladies' Day, if women make a resolve to change, men will also change. Women should take the correct path, then men will also follow suit, as it is the women who have to take the leading role. The wife is half of the husband; if she becomes good, then her husband, who is the other half, will also become good. Women should inculcate qualities of compassion, love and sacrifice. There is no nobler quality than sacrifice. Look to the women of the past. How much compassion they had; how much peace and joy they gave to others; what purity and bliss they had. Because of that, they have become immortal. Even today, they are remembered for their outstanding values and qualities.*

*Therefore, with the hope and blessings that you will behave in the right manner, take a leading role in the affairs of the country and the world at large, and set the proper and right example for others. I bring this discourse to a close.*

The First Ladies' Day Discourse
Prasanthi Nilayam, November 19, 1995

# CHAPTER 7

# MAN'S ROLE : WOMAN'S ROLE

We now turn to some of the qualities, characteristics, and roles of men and women that Sai Baba has taught us. It is historically sound to say that in the past men have been the provider of supplies for our everyday living and women have implemented the usage. Men traditionally earned the income and women used it to provide the necessities for the family's survival. Therefore men can be thought of as the couple's outer image because that was their *primary* area of work, outside the home, and women can be thought of as the inside image, because working inside the home was their *primary* area to work.

What does primary role mean? The role that God created for males and females. Each role is distinct and compliments the other. Primary, simply means that this is your basic nature, your *gift*. These roles are more natural to you. It is *easier* for you to perform your predominant role. It does not mean that you as a female or a male will not crossover and use the qualities of the opposite sex, but Swami teaches us that each gender has a basic nature harmonizing our tendencies that is easier for us to use. You can use the opposite energy, but, in general, it takes more effort to develop.

Even though men and women share duties and crossover into each others' traditional roles, the primary responsibility of the male is to support his family and the women are to nurture the family. The following chart summarizes the primary roles taught by Bhagavan.

| MALE (LAW) | FEMALE (LOVE) |
|---|---|
| **RULES** | |
| OUTSIDE HOME | INSIDE HOME |
| **PROVIDER** | **USER** |
| FOOD | FEEDS |
| EDUCATION | SUSTAINS LIFE |
| SHELTER | NUTURES |
| MEDICAL | PEACE MAKER |
| **WISDOM** | **DEVOTION** |
| DISCIPLINE | LOVE |
| LAW | MODESTY |
| AUTHORITY | TEACHER |
| RULES | SACRIFICE |
| PROTECTOR | VIRTUOUS |

Swami teaches us that the primary male energy is wisdom and the primary female energy is devotion. Now before there is any conflict in your mind, let me say that women have wisdom and men have devotion. But men represent wisdom and women devotion.

*"Women are the fountain-source of love. Devotion is considered a feminine quality while wisdom is considered masculine. Let me not be misunderstood if I say that for the presence of all the male devotees present here, women alone are responsible. It is they who by their sacred feelings brought their menfolk here. Their work is sacred in every respect. They seek not only to sanctify their lives but the lives of all others in the family."* SS December 1996 pg. 326

Men are symbolic of wisdom, they are concerned with the outside world. This is where they spend most of their time. Women are responsible for the work within the home. Man learns wisdom from his outside experiences, symbolic of male energy; devotion is developed from within, female energy. When these two energies marry, the male and female, they represent two halves of a balanced whole, each symbolic of our two images, the inner and outer. We each use both images, outside and inside, but one will predominate over the other, depending on our sexual identity.

We marry opposites; this is the law of attraction. In marriage we can closely observe each other and learn to develop the opposite qualities. Men who work outside the home are responsible for teaching the children about the rules and laws of society. Subjects concerning politics, taxes, justice, economics, protection, safety, laws, discipline and worldly communication are predominately in the male domain. These subjects are concerning the world outside the home and interest men.

On the other side of the picture, women are responsible for teaching the children to love God within and without, love and communicate with each other, nurture and develop peace, to share and help each other: all qualities that strengthen our inner image. In general, the behaviour that is taught by the female is love and devotion. The behaviour that is taught by the male is discipline and wisdom. Through these, we teach our children the important aspects of our two energies, the inside and outside world of being human. God's design is perfect.

## MALE AND FEMALE ENERGY REQUIRES BALANCING:

The objective is to balance the male and female energy, not only in our relationships, but also within the individual. In marriage we can learn from observing each other. This gives us a unique opportunity to imbibe the characteristics of the opposite energy.

It is interesting to observe what interests men when they communicate. Men usually discuss politics, sports, work, — anything but the personal problems that might confront them. In our society this is acceptable behaviour, and I believe it is also a part of their nature.

Women on the other hand are more interested in intimacy and personal conversation. They want to speak about their feelings; they want to understand their spouse and to understand their children. Relationships are formed and evolve primarily with what is communicated from within; if there is a problem, most women want to resolve it by mutual sharing on the inner level. They want to remove obstacles that prevent family togetherness. Harmony in the home is usually their top priority.

Sai says, *"It does not matter, how bad or low the husband is, the wife must through love, bring him round and correct him and help him gain the blessings of the Lord."* Golden Age pg. 143

Women, in general, are more natural communicators than men, and so the responsibility of encouraging verbal exchange is in their sphere of influence. Women become very frustrated with their families when there is little or no communication. This is really the women's work area. They cultivate the inner world.

Now, please don't think that I am stereotyping the sex'es. Definitely not. I believe that these roles are God's design. In general, the basic nature of each sex is easier and requires less effort to develop and use. Still it is equally important that we learn both aspects wisdom and love.

Previous generations rarely exchanged gender roles. I think we are ready to balance these energies within ourselves. We are now working in both images, the outside male oriented and the inside female oriented. The crossover or exchange of roles is apparent in today's society and is more the norm now than in previous generations.

Charles Smith, from Kansas State University gives us four traditional roles or popular images of fathers in today's society:

**THE WALLET:** This father is preoccupied with providing financial support for his family. He may work long hours to bring home his paycheck and does not take an active part in caring for the children. Making money provides this father with a distraction from family involvement.

**THE ROCK:** This is a "tough" father, strict on discipline, in charge of the family.

He too may believe that a good father remains emotionally distant from his children, so expressions of affection are taboo.

**THE DAGWOOD BUMSTEAD:** This father tries to be a 'real pal' to his children, but his efforts are often clumsy or extreme. He doesn't understand his children and feels confused about what to do. He may also feel that he is not respected within the family.

These traditional stereotypes are now clashing with a newer image of a father:

**THE CAREGIVER:** This father tries to combine toughness with tenderness. He enjoys his children but is not afraid to set firm but fair limits. He and his wife may cooperate in childrearing and homemaking.

Dr. Smith also says, "This shift in the caregiver role is influenced by two major social changes: the increase in the number of women working and the rising divorce rate. As more and more mothers join the work force, fathers are being asked to take on more responsibilities at home."

Isn't this encouraging! I have watched the young fathers taking an active part in raising the children and helping with the household chores. It is quintessential that the husband

and wife both share in all the duties and responsibilities. Anger, frustration, and resentment create arguments; if you observe this in a spouse, check that it is not caused by an imbalance of the workload. This adversely affects the energy of the entire household. The distress passes from one to the other, especially if it is unacknowledged. I used to say, "If my husband came home and yelled at me, I would yell at the kids, they would yell at each other, and someone would kick the dog!" Somewhere along the way, someone has to break this chain with understanding and love.

All this adds to the existing stress load of this clamouring twentieth century. Communication is the key. Work on yourself, talk, compromise. You need to help each another parent intelligently. With the stressful demands of our shrinking planet, it is not easy, but it can be fun. It simply requires both parents working together.

Swami says, *"It is nowhere stated in any sacred text that woman should only cook and not work like men. As a matter of fact, even men need to learn cooking and housekeeping to help their wives in times of need. Awareness is life. Awareness means total knowledge, not partial knowledge."* Discourse Kodaikanal Women's Day April 19 1998.

We and our children will both benefit with a wise balance of male discipline and female nurturing. When they are equally applied by both sexes our children as well as ourselves will benefit. I remember that enforcing discipline fell to my lot, and the children thought that I was the "heavy". My husband was more lax with the children. This created a "playoff" between parents, a tactic quickly learned by most children to get what they want. If Dad is easier on homework, they will ask him to check it. Or they may ask, "Mom, can I go out tonight to Janet's house?" I would reply, "Go ask your father for approval." The child would go to my husband and say, "Mom said I could go out tonight, is it all right?" The next thing I knew the child was gone, and I would ask Robert, "Where is the child?" But there was little direct communication between Robert and myself. The child said, "Mom said it was OK, can I go?" If I said it was OK, Robert would usually agree. He left most of these decisions up to me. This could create a 5 minute "who-said-or-did-what" argument between us. We needed a method to eliminate these domestic manipulations. Our children were "parent smart" and at a very early age!

We decided that in the future we would, whenever possible, make all the decisions jointly. We would in the future not send any child to deliver messages for us, but ask each other in person. We simply said, "We have to ask mom or dad", whatever the case may be. This also gave us time to think.

Many times the children would ask permission to do something when I was on the phone or their father was watching television. They are very smart. And when I was talking, sometimes I paid little attention to what they were asking, and found myself saying "yes", when I did not know what I was saying yes to. I just wanted time to myself or to visit with a friend. This got me into trouble. Now I had a pat reply, "I'll discuss it with your father, later." It was a struggle at first to implement, but soon the children got the message: we were no longer divided but unified. This takes practice.

Baba told us in Kodaikanal, *"Practice, practice, practice, spirituality takes practice the same as riding a bike."*

Dr. Smith's research shows: "Children both admire and fear their father's strength. On one hand they want their father to be strong and powerful (in the sense of being self-confident and determined), but they may also be frightened at times by that power. Walking the middle ground between dominance and permissiveness can sometimes be difficult for a father.

"How can fathers establish a sense of influence? First, they can establish and maintain reasonable limits for their children. Research has shown that delinquent boys are likely to have fathers who are controlling, rigid, and prone to alcoholism. These fathers may use physical punishment as a form of discipline, and they tend to be inconsistent and erratic in their childrearing techniques. Children respect parents who provide firm but gentle guidance. But they also benefit from parents who gradually allow them to make decisions on their own."

Swami says, *"Parents, do not set a good example to the children. In the modern age, the father does not correct the child, and the child does not listen to the mother. Therefore 90% of the fathers are like Dhritarashtra; they will accept anything that their children do. This is the reason why the world has come to such a sorry state."* SS November - December 1995 pg. 294

Dr. Smith says, "Fathers could also be responsive to their children's interests. Instead of always telling them what to do, fathers could listen and be responsive to their children's suggestions whenever possible. When shopping, for example, a father might let his 5 year-old choose one or two stores to visit. Similarly, a father might ask his son or daughter to suggest a game to play.

"There are times, though, when children do not have these kinds of choices. Parents often have to have the final word. The goal might be to achieve an appropriate balance of influence in the relationship.

"When people feel accepted and respected in a relationship, they will begin to develop close feelings of mutual affection. Parents who are never involved with their children and are either too permissive or too dominant are not likely to become close to their children. Fathers who expect to be constantly vigilant disciplinarians who show no tenderness create a climate of coldness that puts distance in their relationships. Sometimes the effect can be painful." "Fathers Care" Document by Dr. Charles A. Smith October 1996 Kansas State University, Source of Research. Michael Lamb, The Role of the Father in Child Development (New York: John Wiley, 1981)

We must evolve to the stage where we can inculcate both these energies, love and discipline, in a balanced and harmonious style.

One way to judge whether we are becoming more balanced is to look at our relationship with our spouse and see if we are sharing household duties, as well as love and discipline with our children. "Working women spend 3 hours a day on housework and 50 minutes a day with their children, while men do 17 minutes of housework, and spend 12 minutes with their children." Joint Study between the World Health Organization and Melbourne based Key Center for Women's Health in Society.

Our lifestyle can be symbolic of our need to balance one of these energies within ourselves. The expansion of male and female energy within each of us, is an example to our children. It can accelerate their ability to balance their own energies. Furthermore they will have an easier time adjusting when they get married. The cross-over will come naturally.

Sai Baba says, *"Love the children, but give them stern correction if they do anything wrong. Timid parents of today fear to establish strict rules for the children, as they think the children may run away from home or end their lives."* SS November December 1995 pg. 294

# CHAPTER 8

# TEACHING SELF-DISCIPLINE TO CHILDREN

Have you ever thought that if we don't tell our children, "**No**," how will they ever learn to tell themselves **NO**? **Stop** and think about this, it is very important.

Swami says, *"Parents have the primary responsibility to molud the character of their children."*

The character is moulded through our example, instruction, love and discipline. The subject of discipline has been continuously emphasized by our Beloved Baba.

He says, *"Ninety percent of the blame for spoiling the behavior and character of children, go to the parents. They show too unintelligent affection and give too indiscriminate a freedom to them."* SS January 1994 pg. 24

Why is discipline so important? Because we would not even get out of bed in the morning without discipline. It is the function of the conscience that tells us to STOP. To stop sleeping too long, eating too much, crying too long etc., etc. It is the conscience mechanism that controls our behavior. Would you put your child in a car without a brake? Can you imagine yourself driving a car without a brake? It is the same with our behaviour; discipline is the brake. The car is our body, our action, our personality. As of now, the children are driving their bodies without using the brake of discipline. They are out of control. Their behavior is not in accordance with Swami's teachings.

Now, what we are seeing in the Western culture is children who control their parents. In a way, the children are ruling the parents, instead of the parents governing the children. This is not a correct situation.

Sai says, *"The parents are to blame for three-fourths of their children's behaviour. When parents allow the children to go astray, sometime or other they will suffer the consequences. It has become fashionable in the Kali Age to let the children have their own way. The parents give a free rein to the children instead of controlling them."* S S May 1996 pg. 120

Our parents' generation experienced the greatest advancement in technology. They had neither indoor plumbing, electricity, nor cars when they where children. Imagine the changes they witnessed in the material world alone.

In my opinion, our generation has seen the greatest *"annihilation of morality."* We have experienced the great revolution of immorality. Many of the values that existed for our parents are non-existent today. We have had to emotionally and psychologically accept *what is* while longing for our memory of family values that once existed. Divorce was the rare exception and only for extreme cases.

Swami says, *"When materialism goes up; morality goes down. When morality goes up; materialism goes down."*

This is our dilemma. Our society has lost its moral fiber because of its focus on enhancing our physical life with more and better products, as well as pleasing ourselves, fulfilling desires, irregardless of spiritual expense. What has happened to the moral strength gained by the struggle to overcome difficulties which sustained the pioneering spirit of the older generation? We live in such physical comfort that our children are pampered into indolence. It has cheated and impaired their spiritual character. Spoiling them has made them weak. They do not know how to fight for survival. We have certainly failed them.

Because of the industrial and technological age, we became consumers of comfort and pleasure. We wanted our children to have everything. We watch the commercials on television, followed their advice, and bought and purchased and consumed ad nauseum. We discovered that happiness couldn't be purchased for ourselves or our children. You can't buy happiness, period. The children only want more......why? Because we did not teach them or ourselves how to apply the brake of self-discipline.

We are programmed to be consumers. We have bought into the marketing strategy, hook line and sinker. We work, work, and work. Why? To have a higher standard of living? Do we really need as much as we have? When we keep purchasing goods, we are teaching our children by our example to continue the same behaviour. The manufacturing companies love it.

Swami says, *"Waste of money is evil, teach children not to receive anything for nothing. Let them earn by hard work the things they seek."* SSS # 2 pg. 192

Love and discipline have been replaced by purchasing power. We buy items to tell our children how much we love them. We reward our children with gifts if they study, do a chore, or correct a negative behaviour. We are controlling them with rewards, physical rewards, not teaching them the self - discipline that rewards the child by building their self-esteem. It is the inner reward that counts. People need character to sustain themselves.

Just think about yourself. Don't we all want to earn our own way? We seek independence, not dependence. Often, people find receiving more difficult than giving.

But we are not teaching our children to give, thus we have a "me" generation, with very low self-esteem.

One night, Swami gave me an insightful dream. I was struggling to understand the cause of the "me" generation. In the dream Swami told me that my generation, the first to raise children with television, was unknowlingly subconsciously programmed by the commercials on television. All of the commercials were targeted for parents who had the money to buy items for their children and family. For example, only the best detergent for diapers, the best baby food, the best products for cooking etc. Every household had been subtly programmed to create *parent* peer pressure, in addition to the peer pressure created for our children. If the neighbour's child gets a Barbie Doll that was advertised on television, the other parents in the neighbourhood felt obligated to do the same for their child. The same peer pressure is extended in countless ways. For example: birthday parties, dancing lessons, sports events etc.. Rarely on television are the children programmed to give to the parents.

In previous generations, children were trained to help. The parents taught the children to support them and to be grateful for their parents. They learned to help them grow crops, take care of the small children, do chores, assist in the family business etc. The emphasis was on the children helping the parents. In this modern age of material comfort, the emphasis is on parents doing everything for the child. Very rarely do you see anything on television, in the commercials, films or sit-com's that addresses the issue of children helping and respecting their parents? How are they to learn? How do we stop this avalanche of self-centredness instead of selflessness?

Swami says, *"Apart from educational programs, do not look at television at all, especially while taking food. Concentrate on the work at hand, whether it be eating or anything else."*

Since parents are responsible for developing the character of their children, it is our duty to teach them the joy of giving to others. Few are going to teach them in our western society. We parents must take the reins.

How can we do this? When the children are very young, we talk to them about the joy of giving to others. The small child can bring the newspaper for dad to read, the diaper for the new born member in the family, the napkin for grandma's lap, the cookie for a friend. This is character development. The emphasis is on the child helping first its parents, then their family members and friends which eventually extends outwardly into society ending in service to God, and service to man is service to God.

The husband and wife set the example by giving to each other. The child will observe and learn. But example is never enough. Teaching must also be there; speak Swami's truths and use discipline to influence the behaviour that is desired.

If the child will not bring a napkin to the grandparents, then you tell them why they need to help others. *"We can only give love through serving others,"* says Swami. It is the joy and love that we extend to others that brings true happiness or union with God.

Now a small child many not understand what you are teaching, but you're planting seeds to program his sub-conscience with Swami's wisdom; you are creating and developing his future behaviour. If your emotions express joy while you are explaining, the child will respond to the emotion. If the child does not comply, you will need to correct the behaviour with some form of discipline.

Swami says, *"Discipline means the observance of certain well-designed rules. Without such regulation it is not possible to maintain humanness."*

# CHAPTER 9

# BALANCING DISCIPLINE AND LOVE

There are two subjects that Swami speaks on frequently which need to be addressed in a comprehensive manner: discipline and outside influence. I intend to cover these two subjects in more than one chapter because they are important. We need to change our indulgent parenting style that permits children to control us, and we need to counteract outside influence that creeps into our households. I am convinced that if we enforce discipline, remove television from our households and monitor the internet, our children will be morally stronger and our job will be easier.

Sai says, *"The younger generation is being ruined by undesirable films and television programs. Their minds are being poisoned. It is not a sign of parental love to let children be ruined in this manner. Even parents should avoid going to cinemas. All the crimes and violence we witness today are*

*largely the result of the evil influence of films on young minds."*
SSS #3 pg. 60

Dr. John Gray, author of "Children Are From Heaven" says in an interview, "Soft parenting is how the children of post World War II reacted to their parents' strict techniques. They realized what their parents did to raise them did not work. So, when they had children, they did the opposite. By doing so, it created a generation of weak-willed parents who lost supervision over their children. Those children ruled the roost. Teens today are completely out of control. It's not fashionable to control your kids anymore. This builds resentment between parent and child. I support parental control by nurturing. If we don't have management techniques, and teach parents how to deal with their children, there will be violent results. That's why there is more domestic violence today. There is no fear of punishment."

It is sad to see children controlling their parents. However, I must say, the children today are old souls that are extremely strong - willed. One father told me that he could not get his 8 - year old son to bed at 9 p.m. unless he himself turned off the television and went to bed. His son said this, "I have learned in Sai Spiritual Education class that you should be an example to me, so if I have to stop watching television and go to bed, so must you."

The father was seeking help. I tried to imagine myself giving my father this order and it just would never have happened. My father would never have permitted that kind of behaviour; but now, children are allowed the upper hand.

I explained to the father, that he is the **Father**. Yes, we must be an example of Swami's code of conduct, but it is not the job of the child to dictate your behavior. There are differing house rules for parents and children. The father has every right to watch the late night news on television while his son is in bed. His child was controlling him.

You are the one that must control your children. Set a time for bed. If your child does not obey then he/she must suffer the consequence. Fathers must take their role seriously for God has empowered you to be in-charge. You and your spouse can set house rules and if they are broken, you determine what discipline you will give to enforce the rule. It's really just common sense, isn't it?

What does Swami say, *"While there is a lack of fathers who can guide their children on the right path and set before them some lofty ideals, some parents preach high ideals, but they cannot correct their own children at home. Who will listen to their sermons? It is easy to speak but difficult to practise."* Sathya Sai Newsletter Summer 1996 pg. 30

Dr. Gray was asked, "Is it good to be your child's friend?" He answered, "No. I am completely against it. The parent is the child's boss. Parents should not seek to placate a child. A parent does not share his feelings with a child. If you do, you lose power. A child is not your peer. You are the boss. When they are age 13 to 18, they are trying to earn their freedom. You need to be their boss and lead with love so they are happy to follow you."

Some working mothers have told me, "I'm with my child so little that I don't want to spend it disciplining them. I'd rather be their friend, I want to spend our quality time doing something together that is fun. It takes so much energy to correct my child and enforce discipline. I'm too tired to deal with it."

Sai says, *"Parents lavish too much affection on their children. There should also be control. There should be both love and law."* SSS # 3 pg. 60

It is not easy to spend the only hours you have during the day with your child, confronting their problem. Quality time can never replace all the time, but if this is the only time that you have to correct their behaviour during the day, then it is your duty to do so.

How do we define quality time? Is quality time defined as pleasing the child? According to Sai, parents have the primary responsibility to mould the character of their children. This is the **quality** that Sai expects from parents....**time** spent in preparing them for their role in life.

One of the Professors from The Sathya Sai Institute of Higher Learning asked Sai Baba one day, "Swami, why do you give the college boys more attention than the girls from the Anantapur College?" Swami replied, *"The boys will get more attention than the girls because of their role in life. I am preparing the girls for their role in life."*

Swami's words echoed in my thoughts, "prepare them for their role in life". This is a clearly defined goal for parents raising children. I was just trying to survive from day- to-day when I was taking care of our children. This phrase helped my mind to focus on the big picture. Are we preparing our children for their role in life?

Are we teaching them that their actions are the building blocks for integrity, responsibility, honesty, honour, respect, humility, the qualities that are important for their spiritual progress and self-esteem? If they do not learn to suffer the consequences of their own actions and expect you to cover-up their mistakes, they will spiritually stagnate. This lesson needs to be taught from birth. If you wait until they are teenagers, you'll find that you're sometimes trying to control a loose cannon!

We have students who find college too difficult and want to quit. Dad and mom can support them. We have adults who find their job uninteresting and leave before they have found another one. We have spouses wanting a divorce because they are unhappy, and don't "love" each other any more. We have children being abandoned because the parents don't want the responsibility. This behaviour we must remedy and prevent in the next generation. With a strong loving disciplinary regime.

Swami says, *"Discipline trains you to put up with disappointments, you will know life has both ups and downs."* SSS # 3 pg. 60

Dr. Gray was asked, "What type of parenting technique do you suggest?"

"The hard-love approach - no screaming, no yelling, no hitting. There is a way of making your child want to cooperate. Parents need to improve communication and connect with their kids. Then children will listen to parents and feel connected so they are willing to cooperate." Interview given to the St. Louis Post-Dispatch Sunday September 5, 1999

97

There is a chart in the Parents Magazine, October 1999, *Discipline for Your Little Ones* by Lori Miller Kase that covers the disciplinary styles of this century, which I found interesting.

## A Century of Discipline Styles

### 1900 - 1920s

At the start of this century, the prevailing wisdom favored a harsh and punitive discipline style to keep kids in line. "Children were seen as bundles of bad impulses that needed to be controlled," explains Irwin Hyman, Ed.D. of Temple University, in Philadelphia. "Children were thought to be literally susceptible to the devil, and parents had to beat the devil out of them."

### 1930 - 1940s

In the 1930 and '40's, parents began to listen to the scientific experts for child-rearing advice. Behaviorist John B. Watson, one of the first parenting experts, believed that children could be conditioned like Pavlov's dogs. He counselled parents never to hug and kiss their children or let them sit on their laps for fear of spoiling them.

### 1950s and 1960s

Pediatrician Benjamin Spock's *Baby and Child Care*, the child-rearing bible of the '50s and '60s, was a welcome change from the rigidity of earlier decades. Dr. Spock assured mothers that responding to their infants' cries would not result in spoiling. He emphasized the individual differences between babies, noting that strict feeding schedules and early toilet-teaching were often inappropriate.

**1970s and 1980s**

Spock opened the floodgates to a more permissive style of parenting that prevailed during these decades. Many parents focused on a child's feelings and his sense of self-esteem — often at the expense of setting limits.

**1990's**

The '90s have seen a resurgence of tough discipline. Psychologist John Rosemond, a newspaper columnist, says parents should be "benevolent dictators" who teach kids to obey "because I said so." Most experts agree and recommend setting firm limits in a nurturing way.    Parents Magazine October 1999 *Discipline for Your Little Ones* by Lori Miller Kase

Personally, I found this chart interesting for it gave the history of discipline in this century. It gives us knowledge as to where we began and what is present today. We have gone from one extreme to the other: the first 50 years recommending strict discipline and the last 50, permissiveness. Society has learned from these two extremes. This chart does not depict all parenting styles, but these were the general philosophies. I remember that my mom would tell me, "No matter how hungry you became, the Dr. told me that I could not feed you until four hours had passed." She heard me crying a lot. We now realize that neither extreme is helpful, and I find it very interesting that the method that is emerging **now** is one of law *and* love; firm yet nurturing. As Sai Baba teaches us, it is time for us to balance the two.

At what age do we begin to  discipline our children? Are babies too young to be disciplined?  The following information may surprise you because there has been a belief that we should not discipline the small infants and toddlers until they are older.

In the *"Parents"* October 1999 Issue by Lori Miller Kase called *"Discipline for Your Little Ones"* it states:

"Most of us have witnessed the range of discipline styles parents use with their young children. We've all seen the exasperated mom smack a 3-year-old for throwing french fries at McDonald's and the angry dad bellow at a small child for having a tantrum in the toy store. At the opposite end of the spectrum, we've observed parents so oblivious to limit setting that they allow a 2-year-old to yank groceries off supermarket shelves or ignore a toddler who's throwing sand at his playmate in the sandbox. Instinctively, we sense that neither extreme is appropriate, but many of us still wonder, What is the best way to discipline babies and toddlers?

"The question is an important one, because experts say that the disciplinary approach parents use during the first three years of their child's life is critical: It will influence not only how a child learns to distinguish right from wrong but also how well adjusted and self-assured a child will ultimately be.

"What children first learn about limit setting is the cornerstone of their moral development, " says pediatrician T. Berry Brazelton, M.D., who recently teamed up with 'I Am Your Child', a national advocacy organization to educate parents about appropriate discipline for kids, 3 and under. According to Dr. Brazelton, being able to set limits is a parent's "second most important gift to a child," after love.

"Children of parents who are overly permissive are going to have a very tough time learning their own limits, developing self-control, and knowing how to regulate their impulses," he warns. Ultimately, they will have a harder time adjusting to society, beginning when they enter school.

"Conversely, children subjected to overly harsh and punitive disciplinary approaches are likely to suffer psychological harm, says Dr. Brazelton. Not only do these kids develop low self-esteem, but they are also at risk of becoming either timid and self-conscious or rebellious and full of rage."

Sai says, *"Discipline must start from the early years."* SS July 1996 pg. 175

Let's investigate this subject of controlling or disciplining our children. From the time they are born, until they mature, you are their conscience. When they are infants you rush to fulfil their survival needs. They become habituated to your constant response and the behaviour begins. You are giving them what they want. It will not hurt for them to cry themselves to sleep, within reason, if a child is not wet, hungry, or in pain,. You are only interested in their well being, and are protecting them from getting harmed or overly tired. The sooner they learn to trust your judgment and feel secure in your decisions the more cooperation you may have.

As they begin to toddle, their words and actions begin challenging, testing you even more to see if you will allow them to do what they want as opposed to what you want them to do. The battle between your conscience and their desires starts very early. The sooner you let them know who is the boss the less trouble you will have when they are in their teens.

Of course, you cannot discipline a newborn or small infant by time-outs, but you can place limits and have a daily routine. Limit their bed time. If they are not ill, let them fall asleep on their own, instead of rocking or sleeping with them. Let them sleep in their own bed, instead of in yours. Let them play in a playpen for short periods during the day instead of roaming all over the house.

Incidentally, the playpen saved my sanity. Today, a playpen is looked upon as "How can I cage up my child?" Again it is the overly permissive approach, allowing them to roam and do as *they* please. Restricting their movement or behavior has not been in vogue. I used it for short periods of the day, half an hour, and if the child was content playing with his/her toys, I extended the time. They will let you know. I was free to prepare dinner without worrying, "where was this toddler"? The playpen provides the infant's safety and the parent's peace of mind. But today we think how could we be so cruel as to confine our child in a playpen or gated room? Nonsense. It teaches them limits and boundaries.

If you are going to have a child, start immediately with your newborn, letting the child know who is in control!

Here are some examples of "you say / they say" which typically apply in all households.

## The formula is simple: It's YOU versus THEM

| YOU SAY | THEY SAY |
| --- | --- |
| EAT YOUR DINNER | I DON'T LIKE IT |
| TAKE A BATH | I'M NOT DIRTY |
| CLEAN YOUR ROOM | WHAT'S WRONG WITH IT? |
| TIME FOR BED | NOT TIRED |
| TIME TO GET UP | TOO TIRED |
| YOUR LATE | NO CLOCK |
| WHO'S FIGHTING? | HE/SHE IS |
| WHO DID THIS? | NOT ME |
| SHARE YOUR.... | IT'S MINE |
| DO YOUR HOMEWORK | DON'T HAVE ANY |
| YOU CANNOT GO | ALL MY FRIENDS CAN |
| CHANGE YOUR CLOTHES | WHAT'S WRONG WITH THIS? |
| GET OFF THE PHONE | I JUST GOT ON |
| WHAT DID YOU DO | NOTHING TODAY? |
| WHERE IS THE MONEY? | I DON'T KNOW |
| STOP THAT ARGUING | YOU DO! |

Do these answers sound familiar to you? It is really very simple. Look down the centre of the two columns, called **YOU SAY....THEY SAY.** This division is the line of separation that creates our child management problems. God has the same "child management" issues with us. He wants us to give up our ego desires and body identification. We hear the voice of the conscience but we, too, would rather follow our impulses. Our children present us with a similar condition; there is little difference. Always, always look to your relationship with **God**, to determine what your role is as a parent. You are fighting the battle with their ego and it is powerful.

Sai says, *"To earn the goodwill of the Master, there is one recipe; obey His orders without murmur....Grace is showered on all who obey instructions and follow orders."* SSS # 2 pg. 184

I could give you many examples of what <u>they</u> want versus what <u>you</u> want: hours on the phone, not wanting to go to bed, fighting with brothers/sisters, insulting parents, returning home late, watching television, going to movies, not cleaning their room etc. But let us realize that whatever the circumstances, the underlying cause is *always the same,* **"Your will against their will."**

A toddler only knows a few words, but one of the first he catches is **"NO!"** That's plain enough. When they get older they embellish it a little, with phrases as in "you say -. they say" or worse. Its your Will versus their will. You don't need many examples on how to discipline, all you need is to know how to say sweetly, but firmly with love, **NO.** Practise it. If they don't respond then you must enforce it with discipline.

The sooner they learn that your word will not be changed, the easier your job will be, now and in the future. Inconsistency allows them to think they can have their own way. The more you give in...the more they test you. Inconsistency gives them greater control; you loose ground. Your job will become harder each time you give into them. They will continue to beg, plead, scream, throw temper fits, anything to try and persuade you to give into their wish. If they know that you mean **"NO"** when you say it, they will finally get the message and relinquish the struggle to manipulate you. Be consistent! Repetition habituates the behaviour.

Swami does the same with us. If we have a harmful desire or habit He makes our life uncomfortable with this desire, until we let go and surrender it. When we are new to the spiritual path, we often prolong the struggle, wanting the desire fulfilled. The longer you are on the spiritual path, the quicker you let go! You simply learn that "what you want versus what He wants" is a lost battle before it even begins. The same process will work with your child.

Sai says, *"When students do not behave, Swami tells them softly, Bangaru, you don't do that. If they still do not behave, Swami raises His voice. His voice changes but Swami's heart does not change. That you demonstrate."*

Most of us want our children to love us. It is painful when we have to enforce a rule. We don't like to see them hurt or angry. We want to play with them and enjoy their company. The problem is that when they become adults and do not have the ability to control themselves, their suffering increases because the *risks* are larger. And I might add we also suffer when they, for example, leave a job, get a divorce, drink too much alcohol, drive recklessly, or ignore their familial duties. In general, we suffer when they suffer.

A group of devotees from Madras came to Bhagavan and said, "Swami please visit our Centre in Madras?"

Swami replied, *"What is the use? You are not regular in your appointment with God. One day, you commence Bhajan at 5 PM another day at 5:30 PM. When you say that you Commence Bhajan at 5 PM God will always be ready at your door step. But you want to give importance to a guest politician who was to come to attend the Bhajan. Discipline is my Second Name. Remember this."* Swami's talks to Students

Our children wandering away from God would be our ultimate failure. This is the main task set before us....to bring our children to God. If we take our duty seriously, make every effort, and our children fail to realize the God within, then we sigh and ponder their karma. You are not responsible for the results, the good or not so good. You can only execute your duty in the best way that you know. When you have done this, and the results are not what you sought, it is up to God to change what you cannot.

Swami said, *"He alone is the father who tells his son "Child realize God". He is the true Guru, who leads the disciple to God. Such teachers and parents have become rare these days. All that had brought fame and glory to the country in the past has become a waste, because of the decline of the moral values and behaviour. The educational system is utterly vilafied."* Swami's talks to Students

Suffering is a part of life; we must learn to accept it and go on living, and even loving our living. **By placing**

**emphasis on pleasure, we are sending the message that pain is so unbearable that it must be avoided at all cost, we must find an escape.**

As Sai says, *"Pleasure is a brief interval between two pains."*

Our job is to teach them that life holds both joy and grief. The more we stress the importance of one over the other, the lesson of treating them equally is not learned. Yes, I know this is certainly a task for the self-realized, but it is important for us to strive for the ideal. Don't place so much importance on seeking pleasure by continuously entertaining the child. They are so highly stimulated today that they cannot seek the simplicity of enjoying their own imagination. They must even be entertained in the school classroom. Is it too difficult for the child to realize that learning is often hard work, and not always entertaining? is it not the time for entertainment? We are pampering the children too much. We assume they cannot face the reality of life unless we sugar coat each event.

Allow the child to struggle with its own life issues. Our purpose for being in the body is to overcome it, transcend it. If we do not teach them how to face each situation fearlessly, to confront problems and challenges, fighting with a strong will and all their might to overcome the evil forces that are here on earth, then they will succumb. Our conscience is training their conscience, teaching them what is right and what is wrong. This will develop a pattern of behaviour that will sustain them throughout their lives.

Sai teaches us, *"Do good and have good in return; do bad and accept the bad that comes back; that is the law."* SSS #7 pg. 90

If our child makes a mistake, we can teach them how to correct it. This builds their self-esteem and self confidence, which are essential aspects of self-love. Can we continue to deny our children the art of self-discipline, the core of character building, by spoiling them?

Swami says, *"Parents, have the primary responsibility to mould the character of children. Too much freedom should not be given out of excessive affection. Children should be taught to exercise self-restraint and observe discipline in their daily life. If parents are negligent in bringing up the children in their most tender years, it will not be easy to correct them later on."*

# CHAPTER 10

# HARMONY IN PARENTING

**H**armony in parenting is directly linked to how well we teach our children right conduct. We enjoy the company of good children — those who have learned to be kind and polite. Our heart is sadder when we see a rude disobedient or dis-respectful child because this is also an unhappy child.

Correcting negative behaviour is the most difficult job of parenting, but it is the very core, the essence of character building. As a parent, I discovered two obstacles that prevented me from obtaining this goal: Consistency and follow through. Regarding consistency, one day I would correct a child's negative behaviour and the next, I would overlook it. Sometimes I was just too tired or busy, or simply did not want to be bothered with another confrontation. It takes enormous energy to change unwanted behaviour in our children.

Regarding the second obstacle, follow through —
continuously correcting and disciplining a child — just
added to my already too long list of chores: It was sometimes
easier to merely ignore the unwanted behaviour.

Eventually, I realized that inconsistency and lack of
follow through wouldn't make the problem go away. Life as
a parent wasn't any easier for me; the kids' unwanted
behaviour was becoming more and more disturbing and
disruptive to family harmony. I had to face the reality that
the only solution was to be more disciplined myself in
consistently and systematically correcting their behaviour. I
had to find a way that would eventually lead to a new and
better behaviour pattern.

Most importantly, I was failing not only myself but my
children because their negative impolite behaviour resulted
in *pain* for them due to the *rejection* they felt from others.
Being lax did not build good character, self-confidence or
self-esteem. Consistency and awareness of consequences
became my two main strategies for changing my children's
behaviour.

Let's look to Swami to understand consistent parenting:

*"Unity of Thought, Word and Deed is needed. Thoughts,*
*words, and deeds should be in harmony with one another.*
*Normally, people tend to think one way, speak in another*
*and act in yet another. This is unbecoming and hypocritical."*
SS March 1988

Bhagavan teaches us that when our thoughts, words
and deeds are in balance we have harmony. This, of course,
is especially applicable to parenting and the creation of
happier, more balanced offspring. Add the idea of the

<u>consequences</u> of your acts and you have four important, rather sequential ideas. Let's call it the "Harmony Circle." *

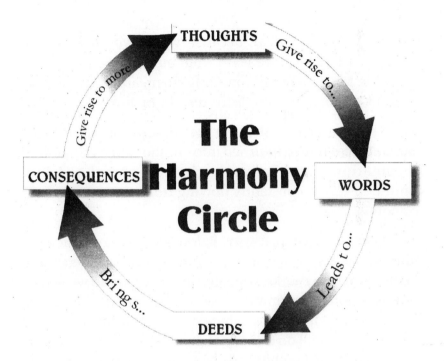

* The framework for this conceptual model initially came together over 30 year ago. Although it differs somewhat from other frameworks (the several EHV models, for example), Swami has on several occasions looked at it and blessed it, advising me to continue with this work. This is of course understandable. To our Bhagavan, all roads lead to Truth, which is Him.

It works this way:  Before we take any action, we first <u>think</u> about it. The seed of the idea begins to form.  Then, we begin to put it into words, in effect, we "give our word." This is our inner decision or commitment to do something. Then we do it, we perform the deed. Finalizing the harmony circle, is the idea of <u>consequences.</u> We received feedback from the world, from others, regarding the <u>consequences</u> of our action.  This is critical, because when we observe and evaluate our actions, we learn from our experiences in life. If we don't, we just keep repeating them, and thus we lose precious opportunities to learn discrimination.

The knowledge that we learn from looking at  the consequences is then returned into our thought bank, adding information.  The harmony circle is completed in a continuous cycle  constantly flowing from one crucial phase to another.

Let's say it another way. Before we take any action the mind thinks about what we are going to do. Experience and learning expand our knowledge,  and every time we decide to take action, we commit  to do (or not to do) something. This decision is in effect a statement of commitment  to apply knowledge. "I will do this or not do this." The 'Word' can be a verbal statement within ourselves or vocalized; nevertheless it is an agreement to take an action. The next step is the actual performance of the act. This step is the experiential learning step in the laboratory of  life.  Action gives us the physical proof we need to see if our knowledge or  information that gave rise to the action was correct.

The next stage is evaluation, and it  is crucial. Examination of our actions is essential for us to improve. If a scientist performs an experiment in a laboratory and does not include an analysis of the results then what is the point of the experiment? It is essentially the same with our behaviour. Examination of our actions is essential for us to improve. We need to ask ourselves: did the act accomplish what was intended? What did I learn? What are the consequences? Were the results of my action positive or negative? How can I improve next time?

The Harmony Circle is a pattern made from Sai Baba's teaching to check and continually improve our behaviour. Are our thoughts really in agreement with what we are saying and then, are we doing as we are saying?

We can use this model to help imbue our children with consistent behaviour and make them responsible for the consequences of their actions, thereby developing their character.

## FIRST STAGE HARMONY CIRCLE PROCESS - THOUGHTS

Getting the thoughts straight is important. We need to clearly instruct our child as to what it is we want him/her to learn or do and give the reason. For example: "Please clean the garage after school. Sweep it out and put the bicycles on the side so we can get the cars inside (the reason). This would be a great help."

Thus we are at the level of thought. We teach children by giving them the information and the reason for our decision or request. This helps them to think, reason, discriminate, and learn. Try to include Swami's teachings as often as possible as this links it to Him and supports your request. Be aware that you are programming their subconscious mind, as well as their thoughts, even when the child is very young. Example: "I am feeding you because I love you and I want you to be healthy and content. Swami tells us, 'Help ever; hurt never'." Try to fill the child's mind with Swami's knowledge rather than the mixed signals that come from worldly commotion. And remember: "communication is always two ways," all is transactional. This helps the child, and helps you to be certain that the child understands what it is you are saying or asking.

## SECOND STAGE IN THE HARMONY CIRCLE PROCESS - WORDS

This step is vital because the child needs to make a commitment. It's not just your decision; their consent is needed for it to stick. Seek to get their agreement (or disagreement) with what you are requesting. Ask, "Will you do this?" Then get a *verbal* response, a "Yes" or a "No". This is very important. If they remain silent, assume there is no agreement, but there is only your word. There is probably no commitment on their part; there is no "contract" between you both. There is information in their silence. Their ego tells them, "Mom or dad told me to do this; but I didn't say I *would* do it so I don't have to."

Gaining commitment is extremely important for moulding character. No verbal agreement makes it easier for them to wriggle out of it. Thus they probably will not learn the value of their committed word. This stage of the process teaches them to be responsible for their actions. It is the "putting into practice" step that Swami tells us we all need.

Swami says, *"The mind creates the bhavam (feeling or thought) which is expressed through the tongue in words and done by the limbs in action. Human life is a combination of the functions of thought, speech and action.* SS January 1999 pg. 23

# THIRD STAGE OF THE HARMONY CIRCLE PROCESS - DEEDS

The action itself. This is the anchor. When we fulfill what we promised, we feel good about ourselves. If the child cleans the garage, you have taught him/her unity of thought, word, and deed, and this brings peace. It also develops self-confidence as well as self- esteem.

Swami says, *"Without Self-confidence, no achievement is possible. If you have confidence in your strength and skill you can draw upon the inner springs of courage and raise yourselves to a higher level of joy and peace. Confidence in yourselves arises through the Atma, which is your inner reality."*

If they do not clean the garage after consenting to do so, they will, probably feel guilty for not honoring their word as well as for disobeying. If they receive no discipline, they get mixed signals. Disciplining their wrong action relieves their feelings of remorse. Reparation does help erase guilt and it teaches them justice. When the debt is paid, positive feelings about themselves replace the negative ones.

Sai says, *"Whatever you want to achieve, do so by proceeding along the right path. Do not go on the wrong path if you are not prepared to face the consequences of it."* SS April 4, 1999 pg. 22

People often ask, "What if the child doesn't agree?" Disagreement helps because they are communicating what they feel or think. "I don't feel like doing it." This gives you the chance to acknowledge their true feelings and also the opportunity to teach them that they have to learn to do many things they might not feel like doing. Mom says, "Jean, I want you to clean the bathroom." Jean says, "I'm going over to Mary's house, I don't want to." Mom responds, "I know you don't feel like cleaning the bathroom but company's coming and I need help."

Swami says, *'The secret of happiness lies not in doing what you like but in liking what you have to do. That is a great Truth.'"*

Again, it is very important to acknowledge the feelings of others when we communicate. Example: "You don't feel good. You've had a bad day. You look tired. You don't feel like doing your homework." This is Active Listening. You try to feed back to a person what they are feeling, saying, or non-verbally signalling to you. When our feelings are recognized emotional stress can be eased and relieved. "At least someone recognized my discomfort." Then you continue communicating what needs to be done, and clarify what they personally need to do. Whenever possible add Swami's teaching to put it all in perspective and help develop their conscience.

Swami says, *"Parent means 'pay-rent.' Children should pay the rent of respect and service to parents who gave them the room they live in called body."*

## FOURTH STAGE IN THE HARMONY CIRCLE PROCESS - <u>CONSEQUENCES</u>

If the child will not agree to do as asked, give him/her a choice to apply their reasoning and conscience, clarifying the consequences of their acts. "If you don't clean the garage when you come home from school you will be confined to your room (for the next two days). It's your choice: the garage or room?" Make sure you get their answer. In this way you teach them that all of their actions have consequences.

Swami says, *"Today man has attained considerable progress in science and technology, but moral values and righteous conduct are on the decline. He has become a slave of selfishness. Whatever one thinks, speaks, or does is only based on self-interest. Human quality has become rare among men, and animal quality is predominant."* SS January 1999 pg. 22

Children have to see and experience the consequence of their actions. This is how they constructively learn from their own direct experience. If, after making a commitment to you, they do not perform their job, then follow through by disciplining them. Again, this teaches them to be responsible for their actions. Otherwise, they are being taught that they can say one thing but it's okay to do something entirely different. The child learns, "There are no consequences for my actions! I promised but did not deliver and nothing happened. I didn't feel like doing it and I didn't have to." The message they receive is that it's okay to lie, okay to be devious, okay to be irresponsible, and okay to be lazy. Is this what we want to teach?

Swami says, *"It is the duty of parents to set children on the right path from their early years. They should not hesitate to correct them and even punish them when the children take to wrong ways. The best way they can show their love for their children is to do everything necessary to make them follow the right path. If any boy proves intractable or incorrigible, they should not hesitate to disown him. It is better to have one good son, rather than a brood of bad children."* SS March 1984 pgs. 62-63

The Harmony Circle conveys the necessity to harmonize your thoughts, words, deeds, and consequences.   It's easy to remember the stages and if you skip one, correction is easy too.   Ask yourself these four questions:

1. Did I give the correct information?

2. Did they repeat it to make sure they understood?

3. Did they make a verbal commitment?

4. What were the results?

These 4 four energies help you achieve **consistency** in your parenting.

Learning is multi-level and simultaneous.   The Harmony Circle — thoughts, words, deeds, consequences, — develops the skills of using the intellect, conscience, emotions, and  physical body.   Your intellect is helping improve the child's ability to use its intellect, to think, reason, analyze and gain knowledge.   Your conscience is helping develop its conscience.  Your inner guidance is helping the child to listen to its inner voice for guidance. Everytime you make sure that  practise what it had  committed to do, you are helping it  learn obedience to you and to it self, its own word! Obedience will one day be the cornerstone of its relationship with God.

When they (childern) perform the deed they are learning to practice what is committed, and this learning occurs throughout the physical body on all levels. When their intellect, their conscience, and their physical body are in harmony, they have positive feelings, the emotions.  A good learning experience teaches them self-confidence, self- worth, and self-esteem.

Sai says, *"My Sankalpa (divine plan of action) is to provide the youth with an education which, while cultivating their* intelligence, *will also purify their* impulses and emotions *and equip them with the* physical and mental *disciplines needed for drawing upon the springs of calmness and joy that lies in their own hearts. Their higher natures will have to be fostered and encouraged to blossom, by means of study, prayer, and spiritual discipline, and contacts with the sages, saints, and spiritual heroes and heroines of their land, to place them on the path of Self-confidence, Self-satisfaction, Self-sacrifice, and Self-knowledge."* SSS #7 pg. 162

There are several levels of learning involved in the Harmony Circle process. Swami's five basic human values truth, right conduct, non-violence, peace and love are being taught on a subtle level through the Thought, Word, Deed, Consequence model. All roads do lead to Truth. In this particular model **Truth** is being taught through your instruction in the process involved in "Thought." And it is being conveyed through your being an example of Sai Baba's teachings. **Right Conduct** is being taught when you teach your child to apply his/her will — which in this model, comes under "Word", which is clearly linked to performing the action, which is "Deed." **Non-violence** is also being taught when you teach your child to evaluate the "Consequences" of his/her act by asking, "Were my actions harmful in any way?" If the Thought, Word, Deed is one: the child's emotions will register **Peace.**

Sai Baba continually reminds us of the integrated nature of the five values. They are not separable." He says, *"The enumeration of human values as five - Truth, Right Conduct, Peace, Love and Nonviolence - is not correct. They are all facets of foundational humanness. They grow together; they are interdependent, they are not separable. Dharma, for example, is love in action; and love thrives on inner peace, on the absence of inner conflicts. How can one have peace when one revels in violence of speech and action?"* SSS #6 pgs. 158-159

**Love** is the value that is within all values.

Swami says, *"The principle of love is the most important of all. Love is Atma; love is wisdom, love is truth; love is righteousness; love is peace; love is nonviolence. Where there is love - - untruth, violence and restlessness find no place."* SS September 30 1998

## The Harmony House of Human Values

The Harmony House of Values is a home of truth, peace, right conduct, love and non-violence. Truth is the very foundation upon which we build a spiritual home. The structure that rises from the foundation is supported by walls of inner strength which are built according to the code of Right Conduct. The walls are the boundaries, the limits and the rules that give strong support to the house. Inside the home dwells inner Peace. The roof covers and protects this spiritual home from physical, mental, emotional and spiritual harm, it is the shield of Non-violence. Love is everywhere!

Self-confidence, Self-satisfaction, Self-sacrifice, and Self-realization naturally evolve and flower in Swami's Harmony House!

# THE HARMONY HOUSE
## OF
# HUMAN VALUES

LOVE ENCOMPASSES IT ALL-ITS ABOVE US, BELOW US,

**ROOF:NON-VIOLENCE**
*PROTECTS THE FAMILY FROM HARM*

WALLS REPRESENT RIGHT CONDUCT

**INSIDE:**
**PEACE**
**DWELLS**
**WITHIN US**

-THE RULES-THE LIMITS
-THE BOUNDARIES

**FOUNDATION:THE TRUTH**
**THE BASIS OF LEARNING RIGHT CONDUCT**

& ALL AROUND US

# GOD IS LOVE

# CHAPTER II

# PREMA AND THE TRIPLE PURITY

## DIVINE DISCOURSE

*E*mbodiments of divine love! He who recognizes that the Aathma in him and in all beings is one and the same, wells in the constant presence of God, whether he is a householder or a renunciant, whether he is alone or in a crowd. Everyone has to recognize the divinity that is inherent in all human beings.

The sage Naarada declared: "Prema amrithasya svaruupah" (Love is the embodiment of ambrosia). In the mundane world, man considers the four Purushaarthas (the four goals of life) as the means to Moksha (Liberation). This is not correct Dharma (Righteousness), Artha (material wealth), Kaama (the satisfaction of desire) and Moksha (Liberation) which are considered the four aims of human existence, are not all. There is a fifth aim for mankind which transcends even Moksha (Liberation). This is Parama-Prema (Supreme love). This Love Principle is Divine.

*Love and God are not distinct from each other. God is love and love is God. It is only when the truth of this Love Principle is understood that the meaning of human existence can be realized. Says a Telugu poem:*

> *The Sai Lord is the embodiment of Love,*
>
> *Who taught the Love principle,*
>
> *Proclaimed the equality of all beings,*
>
> *And revealed the preciousness of humanness.*

*In a home where three persons live, if they have harmony amongst themselves and cooperate with each other, verily that home is heaven itself where divine bliss reigns. If, on the contrary, the three persons lack harmony and adjustment, dislike each other and behave as enemies, there can be no hell worse than that.*

### Ancients considered triple unity as a form of yoga

*Heaven and hell are dependent on the conduct of people. The body is a home wherein reside three entities called manas (mind), Vaak (speech) and limbs (organs of action). True humanness consists in the unity of thought, word and deed. In Vedaantik parlance, this unity was described as Thrikarana Shuddhi (triple purity). True moksha (liberation) consists in giving expression in words to the thoughts which arise in the mind and to practise what one says. The ancients considered this triple unity as a form of yoga. "Manasyekam, vachasyekam, karmanyekam mahaathmaanam" (Those whose mind, words and deeds are in complete accord are high-souled beings). "Manasanyath, vachas-anyath, karmanya-anyath dhuraatmanaam" (The wicked are those whose thoughts deviate from their words and actions).*

*Hence every man should strive to achieve unity in thought, word and deed. That is the hall-mark of humanness. This profound* truth is proclaimed by the Vedaanthik pronouncement that the body is a temple in which the eternal Aathma is the Indweller.

The Veda is dualistic. Vedaantha is monistic. (Advaitha). The essence of Vedaantha is the triune unity of thought, word and deed. In this unity, true bliss can be experienced.

It will also demonstrate the spiritual basis of divinity.

**Vedhaanta is of no avail if precepts are not practised.**

There are today countless numbers of scholars who expound the Vedaantha and they have numerous listeners. The outcome of it all is precious little. This is because there is no practice of the teachings of Vedaantha. All study of Vedaantha is of no avail if the precepts are not practised.

People have to find out what are the easy methods of putting into practice the Precepts of Vedaantha. The easiest way is to cultivate harmony in thought, word and deed. Here is a Thelugu poem:

> Can the world's darkness be dispelled
> > by talking about the glory of light?
> Can a diseased man's afflictions be
> > relieved by praising panaceas?
> Can a destitute's poverty be relieved by
> > listening to the greatness of wealth?
> Can a starving man's hunger be appeased
> > by descriptions of delicacies?

Rather than listening to a ton of precept, it is better to practise an ounce of teaching.

What we have to practise today is something very easy and very subtle. The spirit of service is the royal path to be followed.

*How is this spirit of service to be cultivated? The Geetha lays stress on the word Suhrith (friend). Who is a true friend? Can he be utterly selfless? Will he help you without expecting any return? Whether it be one's mother, husband, wife or son, they love you for their own selfish reasons. A totally selfless friend cannot be found in the world. It is hard to find anyone who renders service totally without self-interest. God alone is totally selfless as a friend and benefactor. God has been described as Suhrith, a friend who is your alter ego. God seeks no reward of any kind. There is no trace of self-interest in Him. God alone can be utterly selfless and loving, expecting nothing in return.*

### Follow the royal road of God's injunctions.

*If you ask a friend where he is residing, he will give a certain address, but this address relates only to the residence of the body. But the true residence of one is his Aathma (the Self).*

*This Aathma is the embodiment of love. Therefore, you have to dwell in love and live in love. You must dedicate your life to that love. If you devote Your life to the pursuit of impermanent things, you will only get ephemeral things. You must seek what is lasting and permanent. What is it? It is the Bhagavath-Aajna (injunction of the Lord). When you take to the royal road of following God's injunction, you will realize all your desires.*

*You must remember however, that these desires only bind you the more you cherish them. The bonds get reduced when desires are reduced. There must be a limit to desires.*

*Similarly there must be restraint in developing attachments. There is grief when a person dies in a family. Is death the cause of grief? No. It is the attachment to the dead person that is the cause of grief. The process of getting rid of attachment has been described in*

*Vedaanthik parlance as vairaagya. Gradually attachments should be eliminated. In the journey of life the less luggage you carry the greater the comfort you will experience.*

*It may be asked: "How is it possible to reduce attachments and desires in worldly life?" The answer is: "Carry on your business or other activities in a spirit of dedication to the Divine." All actions should be done with the conviction that they are dedicated to the Lord. This is an easy path to follow. Consider all actions as actions performed by the power of the Divine, whether it be seeing or hearing or speaking or doing. Without the power of the Divine, can the eyes see or the ears hear?*

**Divine potency is the source of all talents.**

*The primary requisite for man is to realize the divine potency in him that is the source of all the faculties and talents in him. This is true whether one is an atheist, a theist or an agnostic. No one in the world can get on without this energy. It may be called by different names. Names are not important. The energy is one. It is this divine energy which directs mankind on the right path. Men should strive to recognize the presence of the Divine even in small things.*

*In his speech earlier today Anil Kumar spoke about the Sai Organization. The Sai organizations are carrying on their activities with devotion and dedication. But they do not try to find out what should be the ideal to be achieved. "Are you engaged in this work for your satisfaction or for the satisfaction of the Divine?" This is the question they should ask themselves. In this context an incident from the bible may be recalled. Once a devotee went to Jesus and asked him: "Oh Lord! What is the power by which one can protect oneself?"*

*Jesus replied: "Son! When you love God, that power itself will protect you."*

127

In the Bhagavath Geetha, Arjuna asked Krishna, "What should one do to earn the love of the Lord?" The Lord replied: "You simpleton! You imagine you are loving God. The truth is God is seeking a true devotee."

Crores of people all over the world are in quest of God. But where are they searching for Him? In my view, the very ideal of a quest for God is mistaken. There is no need for you to search for God. God is omnipresent. He is everywhere. Devotees imagine they are searching for God. This is not true. It is God who is in search of devotees. "Where is the devotee to be found who is pure in thought, word and deed?" God is searching for such a devotee.

You need not search for god. God is nearer to you than your mother and father. You yourself are divine. How can you go in search of yourself? This is the mistake you commit. When everything is permeated by the Divine, who is the searcher of the Divine? It is because the world has lacked men who could proclaim this Vedaanthik truth with authentic experience that it has sunk to such degrading levels.

### Best way to love God is to love all, serve all

It is needless to search for God. Verily you are the Divine. Strive to realize this truth. There is a simple and easy way. Have the faith that every human being is an embodiment of the Divine. Love everyone. Serve all. The best way to love God is to love all, serve all.

You must love everyone because God is in everyone. Every human being is a manifestation of God. On the cosmic stage every man identifies himself with the form and name given to him. But he does not realize what is his true form and name.

Last night you witnessed the film in which Anjalidevi acted the role of Sakkubai. In the film she appeared as Sakkubai and not

Anjalidevi. But both are one and the same person. God takes on a human form and appears as a human being. But when the human being recognizes his basic divine nature he becomes the Divine. As long as one thinks he is a mere human, he remains human. But when he considers himself as Divine with deep conviction, he will be transformed into the Divine.

## See the cosmos through the glass of spiritual oneness

Hence, thoughts and feelings determine what you are. Change your thoughts. If you give up your worldly outlook and view the world from the spiritual point of view, the Vishwam (world) and the Vishnu (Divine) will become one. Therefore, change your viewpoint. Instead of altering his dhrishti (vision) man wants to change Srishthi (creation). No one can change creation. It is one's vision that has to be changed.

If you wish to experience oneness, you have to see the cosmos through the glass of Ekaathma-bhaava (spiritual oneness). Otherwise, the world will appear as a bewildering multiplicity because you will be seeing it through the glasses of the three Gunas—Sathva, Rajas, and Thamas. Put aside these three glasses. Wear the glass of Ekaathma-bhaava, the feeling of unity in Spirit. Love is one. The Supreme is One though the wise call it by many names.

The Divine has to proclaim this unity when God comes in human form and lives and moves among human beings. The Divine has no likes or dislikes. He has no distinction of "mine" and "thine". He is beyond praise or censure. How, then, should the Divine (in human form) conduct Himself? Everyone should understand this.

## Swami and devotees

Many bemoan the fact that Swami does not speak to them despite their frequent visits. "Is Swami angry with us?" they ask.

*These are not mental aberrations. They are due to total ignorance. Such questions arise in their minds only when they have not understood Swami's real nature. I have no antipathy towards anyone. I do not hate anyone. All are mine. And I belong to everybody. But in dealing with devotees, I have to behave like a doctor who prescribes a specific diet for each patient. For instance, there is a patient suffering from diabetes. He should not consume sweets. If a devotee feels, "I enjoy sweets, why should the Sai Mother prohibit me from eating sweets?" The answer is that it is for his own good. If Swami did not have the patient's well-being in view, He would let him suffer by giving him sweets. It is out of love for the devotee that the Sai Mother denies sweets to him. Swami adopts these different regimens in the interest of curing the devotees' ailments.*

*There are others with a different kind of grievance. For instance, the students often complain that Swami does not talk to them because He is angry with them. I have no anger towards anyone. Whether you believe it or not, I do not know what anger means. But, occasionally I appear as if I am very angry. This is unavoidable because without such assumed behavior on my part, the students will not heed my words. I tell them to behave in a certain way. Some students heed my words and try to act up to them. Some others go against my injunctions. In such a situation, I have to ensure respect for my words. Of what use is it to speak to those who attach no value to my words? I don't intend to devalue my words.*

*Truth is the life of the plighted word. My words bear the imprint of truth. I cannot depart from truth. I don't speak to those who attach no value to My words. This should be realized by those who complain that Swami does not talk to them. When people heed My words, I am ready to help them in every way and confer happiness on them. I do nothing for my own sake. This is My truth.*

## "Everything I do is for your sake"

The Super-Specialty Hospital has been built at the cost of many crores. Was it for my sake? Similarly, the University has been established by spending crores of rupees. For whose sake? Is it for my sake? This magnificent hall (attached to the mandir) has been erected to protect devotees from heat and rain. Am I sleeping in this hall? Everything I do is for your sake. I am surprised that you do not recognize this. Can devotees be so lacking in intelligence? There is no trace of selfishness in Me anywhere. I have no fear of any sort. Only the guilty man is racked by fear. I have done no wrong to anybody and so I have no fear. But I am subservient to devotees.

Not realizing this truth some people imagine that Swami is angry or ill-disposed towards them. Get rid of such mistaken feelings. Be convinced that whatever Swami tells you is for your own good and act up to it. I gain nothing by your good behavior. I don't lose anything by your misconduct. Because I love you, I do not want you to suffer from the consequences of your misconduct.

## Understand God's Love

Turning to God's love, let me make it clear that 99 percent of devotees do not understand what this prema means. This love is construed in a worldly sense. This leads them astray. The attachment between husband and wife, mother and child, between friends, between kith and kin, all are loosely described as Prema (love), but these attachments are the result of temporary relationships and are by their nature transient. Prema is Thrikaala-baadhyam (Love is that which lasts through all the three categories of time – the past, the present and the future). Such love can exist only between God and the devotee and cannot apply to any other kind of relationship.

It is not easy for you to comprehend the true nature of God's love. You are aware only of worldly attachments which are subject *to ups and downs. What is liable to such changes cannot be called love. True love is unchanging. It is Divine. Love is God. Live in love.*

*Embark on this path of love. You are liable to feel elated over trivial pleasures or depressed over petty losses. God's love is permanent and unvarying. Try to understand that love. How is it to be done? By cultivating the feeling that whatever happens to you, whether pleasant or unpleasant, is for your own good. When you have that firm conviction, the value of God's love for you goes up.*

*Most people feel the boundless joy of God's love as long as they are in the presence of Swami. But this feeling evaporates once they are in the environment of the outside world. You must see that the same sacred environment exists wherever you may be, by carrying your devotion wherever you go and spreading the Divine message to every nook and corner of the country. Chant the name of the Lord wherever you are – in the village, in the street, in every home and in your speech and songs. This is the way to ensure that your love of God remains unshaken and unabated.*

*God derives no benefit from this, as He has no desires. He wants nothing. It is only for your own good. "Uddhareth Aathmanaa Aathmaanam" (Elevate yourself by your own self-effort). Failing to recognize this truth, many people imagine that Sai Baba is holding Akhanda bhajans and celebrating various festivals to glorify is name. They are utterly foolish persons. Sai Baba seeks nothing from anyone. You improve yourselves. Become better. Experience your bliss. Make your lives sublime. Utilize these festivals and devotional activities for this purpose.*

### Sathyam, Shivam, Sundaram

*Embodiments of love! As love is verily your form, manifest it in every way, share it with others. The Lord is the Hridayavaasi (Indweller in the Heart).*

*Sarvabhootha-dharam Shaantham*

*Sarvanaama-dharam Shivam*

*Sath-chit-aananda Roopam Advaitham*

*Sathyam Shivam Sundaram*

*(The sustainer of all beings, Peace incarnate, the Bearer of all names, Goodness incarnate, Embodiment of Being-Awareness-Bliss, the One without a second. He is Truth, Goodness, Beauty).*

*The Greek philosopher Plato – who was the teacher of Aristotle, under whom Alexander studied – declared three things as fundamental verities: Truth, Goodness, and Beauty. These are the same terms as Sathyam, Shivam, Sundaram, used by the Indian sages to describe the Divine.*

*Thus in all religions and philosophies through the ages, these three have been declared as the form of the Divine. Love is the form of the Divine. Dharma (Righteousness) is the form of the Divine.*

## "Mother and motherland are greater than heaven"

*The first impulse that emanated from man was Prema (divine love). All other things came thereafter. Every child that is born develops immediately love for the mother. Every child tries to recognize at the outset the mother and the father. In the same manner every individual should recognize the land of his birth and his Samskrithi (cultural heritage). One's nation and one's culture should be revered as one's parents. The nation is one's mother. One's culture is the father. This profound truth was proclaimed by Rama when he declared: "The mother and the motherland are greater than heaven itself." Love the mother. Love your country's culture. These are the two primary duties of every man. They should be the main aims of life.*

When people follow this path of truth and righteousness, love will sprout naturally in their hearts. All knowledge and scholarship are of no avail if there is no practice of virtue. Practise at least one of the teachings and experience joy.

Embodiments of love! Devotees from East and West Godaavari, Guntur and Krishna districts rejoiced in the celebration of what they described as the Golden Jubilee of the Sai Movement. There is no need to seek a reason for experiencing joy. "Sarvada sarvakaaleshu sarvathra Harichinthanam" (Always, at all times and in all places contemplate on Hari). Make every moment a holy day. Invest every word with the power of a manthra (sacred formula). Sanctify the ground you tread on. Make this the mission of your life. Without wasting a single moment, use all the time you can find to spread the message of the Lord's name to every nook and corner of India.

### Desires can be reduced by chanting God's name

Today we are witnessing corruption, violence, wickedness and malpractices everywhere. The basic reason for all these is selfishness. Insatiable desires are at the root of these evils. By chanting the Lord's name, desires can be reduced, while legitimate wishes get fulfilled.

Sakkubai prayed and yearned to go to Pandharpur for darshan of Paanduranga. She endured all kinds of troubles and indignities and earned the Lord's grace. How can you get God's grace without undergoing trials? You know what severe processes gold goes through from the crucible onwards before an ornament is made. There can be no happiness without pain. When you desire the welfare of someone, you must be prepared to let him face the ordeals which are necessary before he can experience what is good for him. Pleasure and pain go together in this world. In the Geetha the Lord says He is both the Kshetra (the body) and the Kshetrajna (the Indwelling Knower).

*What people have to learn today is to give up attachments to the things of the world and seek the love of God. When one cultivates the love of God, renouncing worldly things becomes as simple as leaving hold of a handkerchief. Clinging to property is difficult. Giving it up is easy when people have understood the meaning of God's love.*

*Let people, wherever they may be, in villages or towns, cultivate faith in God, develop love and share it with one and all. Then they will experience ineffable bliss. Liberation will not come through meditation or penance. When you render service with love, it will become meditation, penance and all else. Love is the fifth Purushaartha, the supreme goal of life. Love is also the panacea for all the ills that afflict society today. Hate is the cause of all ills. Hence hatred should be banished, as declared by the Geetha. Don't give room for any evil feelings in your heart, which is the seat of God. Dedicate your minds to God. In due course, you will merge in the Divine and become one with God.*

Discourse in the Puurnachandra Auditorium
On the evening of 14-1-1995

# CHAPTER 12

# HOUSE RULES

By now you may be feeling a little overwhelmed. Dear God, how can I do all that You are teaching us on parenting? I certainly understand your position. Our Beloved Lord does not expect us to instantly achieve our goals. He has the utmost patience, love and understanding. All we need to do is make an effort. We must make a start, and practise. Practise is the key to success. If we make the effort, our Lord must supply the grace that helps us accomplish our task. He says, *"We cannot even love God unless He wills it."* So pray and ask Him to help you in this endeavour. We will never achieve anything if we criticize ourselves, because we are in reality criticizing God. Take your time, travel at your own pace, but TRAVEL. Don't stop before the goal is reached. Each step that we take on the path towards God will eventually help us to reach our destination. It is the same with our parenting skills.

Swami says, *"Everyone of you is a pilgrim on that road proceeding at your own pace, according to your qualification and the stage reached by its means. The advice that appeals to one of you or applies to one of you might not be appropriate to another, who has travelled less distance or reached a more advanced state."* SSS # 9 pg. 58

This chapter on House Rules will solve many of the household problems and integrate the teachings of Sai. This chapter will require you and your spouse to work together and decide what are your house rules, and if broken, what are the consequences. It will be fun and if you are working together to manage your household in an easier way, this chapter will help.

If you are pregnant and expecting your first child, now that you have a quiet time, use that interlude well to establish with your spouse separate and joint convictions on how are you together going to mould the character of your child. Start immediately, because the influence of spiritual music, prayers, and positive thoughts of love is greater than we think on the unborn foetus. Start by reading Swami's teachings a loud to the unborn foetus.

Sai says, *"Teach the children sacred things and not nonsense verses. In the old days, the first words a child was taught at school were 'OM Namah Shivaya'. What should be implanted in the hearts of our children are sacred names like Rama and Krishna."* SS December 1996 pg. 335

Robert and I use to go out to dinner once a week, where we could have the privacy we needed to talk about these matters. We did not want the children to overhear. We also scheduled into our daily activities time after dinner, to take a walk or sit together sharing what happened in our day, while the older children did the dishes. Thus we helped each other sort out the problems of work and child-rearing, while supporting and uplifting each other with Swami's teachings and love.

Swami says, *"Man today lives as he likes without following any discipline. Discipline is needed in every aspect to maintain the right course of life. A river has two banks. But for this, the river may flow in all directions flooding the fields and villages and causing untold hardship and disaster. If it has banks to regulate the course of flow, it will be useful for irrigation."* SS January 1999 pg. 2

Our children also need boundaries; clear limits can provide security. They actually desire to have this protecting structure. I can recall when I would tell one of my children, no, you cannot go to that party. I would overhear them saying, "My mom and Dad won't let me go." It was almost a relief to have someone to blame it on. Too much choice is overwhelming for them. They need routine, and this is what house rules provide.

**HOUSE RULES WORKSHEET      NAME**

**ACTIVITY                          CONSEQUENCE**

PRAYER

BED TIME (A.M. & P.M.)

HOMEWORK (can be done during the quiet time)

QUIET TIME (select the time of day and how long)

CHORES (daily and weekly)

FAMILY (important to schedule family activities per week, month etc.)

INDIVIDUAL ACTIVITIES (how many alone?)

TELEVISION (what programs, how often per week, day?)

ALLOWANCE (weekly)

This is just a sample. You and your spouse will determine your own house rules. The point is to make the rules as simple as possible, but be specific. If you get too technical or complicated, then they will be hard to enforce. If it is not enforceable, don't write it down. It is better to start with a few rules, that are followed CONSISTENTLY, then many rules which are too often broken.

The time schedule determines the family's daily routine. At Swami's Ashram He has a time schedule that keeps us all moving. There is a time to awaken, line-up for darshan, attend darshan and sing bhajans, time for meals, attending lectures, service time, free time, quiet time, and so forth. The time that you schedule for your children is very important, it structures their day.

When a man retires from his job, he often feels lost. He has lived by a time schedule all his life, and now he finds that there is nothing scheduled for him to do. Many times he gets depressed. 'Idle hands are the work of the devil,' so the saying goes. Learning how to motivate yourself and schedule your own time is not easy to do, especially in our ultra-complex modern world. If it is difficult for an adult retiree, how can we expect our children to effectively schedule their own time?

Swami says, *"Time wasted is life wasted."*

**HOUSE RULE - PRAYER**

Prayer is so very powerful. I was taught to pray by the nuns and priests but somehow over the years lost this emphasis until I met Swami. Dr. Jack Hislop told me the following story:

Swami said to him, *"Hislop, the plane that crashed in Bangalore years ago, could have been saved if one person on the plane had said the 'Gayathri Mantra'."* (This is a powerful mantra that Swami teaches His devotees to chant.).

Sai says, *"Have patience and wait prayerfully. Prayer can bring about the impossible."* SSS # 2 pg. 181

The first and the last segment of time scheduled each day should be for prayer, especially for children. Prayer is simply getting in touch with God. It teaches them to turn towards God at least twice daily and preferably more often, seeking His help with everything they do. It is a way of teaching them to contact their inner voice, the voice of God in them. There is nothing as important as establishing a relationship with their inner Divinity. Once this link is established the child will have a safe place to go, to talk to God and seek His help with every circumstance in his/her life. You are helping the child to establish a personal relationship with God.

Swami says, *"Generally, when anyone is in difficulty, he looks to God for help. It is, therefore, natural for children to pray at the time of their examinations. In course of time, children who have begun prayer to tide over their difficulties will make it a regular habit and pray under all conditions. Our Bal Vikas children should be taught to pray before they begin work (whether big or small, important or unimportant). They should be made also to pray before eating, before going to school, before sleeping, etc. Gradually, the need to pray at all times and under all circumstances will dawn on them. They will take to prayer spontaneously."* SS 1978 pg. 86

## HOUSE RULE - BED TIME

Bed time is such a hassle today. The children are not going to bed at a regular time every night because it is so loosely defined. Swami's ashram specifies 9 PM as lights out for adults. Now we see small children staying up as late as 9 or 10 PM. When this happens the parents never have any time for themselves during the entire day.

When I raised my children, I was firm about bed time: 6:30 PM when they were infants, 7 PM when toddlers; working their way up to 9 PM when in high school. My children went to bed early, and I soon discovered it made no difference whether they went to bed early or late, they generally still awoke at the same time. This early to bed was good for their health and it gave me time to get some of my chores finished. When the children are very young they require all your attention. You are constantly working with them, and so there is little time to complete any project.

## HOUSE RULE - QUIET/HOMEWORK

Swami provides for a quiet time at the Ashram. This helps all of us to focus and center, to quiet our minds. The same is needed for our children who suffer stimulus overload. They need a period to quiet down, which can be accomplished by reading, praying, meditating, homework, writing, working a puzzle, coloring, etc. This becomes an opportunity for the entire family to relax and quiet down. You may want to start with a short quiet time and increase it as the family adjusts. When you present your house rules, please explain to the children that you may be adding rules and extending the time. This leaves the door open for all around adjustment, for you and for them.

## HOUSE RULE - CHORES

Chores are a part of Swami's ashram life. We all need to do some kind of Service. It's good for our children if you schedule some chores into their daily routine. Even toddlers can pick up their room.

I will never forget our youngest daughter when she was 4 years old. I asked her to pick up her toys. She said, "No, I want to go to Mrs. Simple's House." (Mrs. Simple was her Pre-School Teacher who just loved and spoiled her.) She would not pick up her toys and was preparing to go to Mrs. Simple's house. I repeatedly asked her and the answer was always the same. "No". We told her that we loved her and did not want her to leave.

Leaving her toys on the floor we packed a few things for her to go to Mrs. Simple's. She wanted all of her things, but I told her they would have to stay with us. She had her bag packed, Robert pulled the car close to the house and my youngest daughter got in. At four years of age she was running away from home because she did not like the house rules!

Neither Robert nor I knew where Mrs. Simple lived, so Robert drove her around for awhile, telling her how much we loved her and really didn't want her to go. Finally, Robert stopped the car in front of somebody's home. Our daughter didn't know the difference. Robert got out and opened her car door and told her we loved her, but if she had to go and really didn't want to clean her room, she was free to go. The little darling, jumped into her father's arms and decided to come home and clean her room. Robert was so relieved!

The other 3 children were waiting on the porch to welcome her back home. It was a great lesson illustrating the struggle between the power of the willful ego and obedience. At four years old her ego was strongly established. We gambled and allowed our child the freedom to experience her choice and its consequence, not knowing what she would do. With Swami's grace, it worked.

Sai Baba says, *"Serve your parents, Help your mother when she goes out shopping. Do not cause any displeasure to the mother. Be ready to give a helping hand to your father. Don't waste your time in idleness. Engage yourselves in social service."* SS May 1996 pg. 121

Chores give the children the opportunity to serve others. It teaches them how to give and the pleasure of giving. It makes them responsible for a job. Praise them when the job is well done. Always, speak in the positive.

Swami told some students, *"Never say what you did was bad, say it was not good."*

Teach them to care for and help their grandparents and parents by contributing to the family.

You can have individual and family chores, but try to do as many projects as possible with the family. I had a cousin who lived on a farm. The whole family together did the canning, fed the animals and picked the crops. They did not own a television. Each evening after their chores, they all gathered together, played music and sang. Everyday was a time of togetherness and cooperation, and topped off with joyful musical pleasure before sleep. Working together teaches the children that they are a part of a team. Cooperation is so much more important than competition.

Family Service is an integral part of teaching a child to be aware of helping individual family members. We do "service" in the community, but it is often the ego that gets attention much more so than for the service we do inside our home. It is not as easy to give service in the home, because there is usually no special recognition for the ego. Chores done in the home are done with less show.

As the child matures, the parents can include them in Sai Service Projects. One dad told me that he was having a difficult time finding something that he and his teen-ager had in common. He brought him to the local soup kitchen where both worked together, fixing and delivering meals. He and his son then had something to talk about that they shared in common. He said it was just wonderful.

Sai says, *"When you offer milk to a hungry child or a blanket to a shivering brother on the pavement, you are but placing a gift of God into the hands of another gift of God! You are reposing the gift of God in a repository of the Divine Principle! God serves; but He allows you to claim that you have served! Without His Will, no single blade of grass can quiver in the breeze. Fill every moment with gratitude to the Giver and the Recipient of all gifts."* Seva A Flower at His Feet, Grace Mc Martin pg. 175

Service comes in three stages: Community Service, Family Service and Transformation.

Sai Baba says, *"Service: The greatest service that you could render is not outside. You should primarily change, transform. Are you good? Do you speak the truth? Are you righteous in your behaviour? Do you have peace? Do you give peace to others? Do you really love others or like others? These are the questions you have to put to yourself. Are you non-violent in your day-to-day behaviour? Can you claim that you do not dislike any one in your life? The substance of the 18 Puranas is "HELP EVER; HURT NEVER". Do you practise? First Master yourself? Master your mind and be a Master Mind."* Swami's talks to the Students

## HOUSE RULE - FAMILY ACTIVITIES

Concerning family activities, free your imagination! Be creative! You can do so many activities together that are inexpensive and fun. When Robert was a small child, he was to go fishing with his mother, but it rained and so the fishing event was cancelled. Still Mother Bruce had a fine imagination. She packed a lunch and carried it with the fishing polls upstairs to the bedroom. Robert and she sat on the bed, which was her make believe boat, put their fishing poles over the side of the bed and had their picnic lunch together.

We moved from one state to another because of Robert's job. I had a cousin who lived near our newly-bought home. My cousin invited us for dinner and to spend the night because it was our moving day. It began snowing late in the day and continued throughout the night. When we awoke the next morning, the snow had drifted to 12 feet or more! The entire city was snowed in.

Four adults and a total of seven children between us were snowbound for three days. Our creative juices had to flow to keep the children (and ourselves) busy. The children began working on a play: writing it, practising and dressing in costumes created from the household wardrobes. For their stage, we hung a sheet to divide the room. We lined up chairs, popped corn, and served juice. It was marvellous.

The husbands, (which we wives called our second set of children) planned a golf tournament. They took plastic cups, laid them on their sides, under tables and chairs in the rooms with carpet. They charted and designed an 18-hole golf course throughout the house. The "tournament" began after their practice sessions, and the entire family was the gallery; we cheered the men on as they putted from hole to hole.

The most delightful and memorable event for me was the treat that the husbands gave to their wives. At the end of the three days, my cousin and I needed a rest from our husbands and kids, so we locked ourselves in the bedroom. Our husbands telephoned us from the kitchen phone and invited us to dine with them at some elegant sounding, make-believe restaurant. They told us to ready ourselves as they would call for us at a certain time.

The game was on! We dressed in long dresses....spent hours getting ready, laughing our hearts out. The men fed the seven children and made a gourmet dinner for us. At the appointed time, dressed in suits, with white towels over their arms, they knocked on the bedroom door, and escorted us to the formal dining room. The table was set with crystal, china, silver and candlelight. Soft music played in the background. They had prepared a four course meal. This is a good example of using imagination to play, delightfully engaging the entire family without expense, creating activities that are not costly. This type of activity strengthens the family unit with sweet memories.

## HOUSE RULE - ALLOWANCE

The next category on the House Rule Worksheet is allowance payment for doing chores. This teaches your children the value of earning money and how to manage it, as long as you don't put too much in their hand that could be misused. Swami is very strict about spending money as well as where and how it is spent.

He said, *"Teach children not to receive anything for nothing. Let them earn by hard work the things they seek."* SSS #2 pg. 192

I have heard Him say, *"Waste of money is evil."*

I remember in Kodaikanal when Swami gave the students money to go buy big straw hats to wear for posing in photos with Him. He told the students not to go to the big shops in town to purchase their hats, but rather circulate the money by buying in the small stalls around the lake. The small stalls needed the business. I applied this to my own shopping habits. I try whenever possible to help the small stores.

Sai says, *"Children must learn thrift and the proper use of money. When children learn how to use money with care and without waste, the future will be bright."* SSS #10 pg. 180

Swami also said, *"Students, these days when your parents send hundreds of rupees you try to misuse the money. That way you will not be in a position to come up in life. Misuse of money is evil. Don't waste money. Don't waste water. Don't waste food. Don't waste electricity or energy."* Swami's talks to the Students

Television, I will address in the next chapter in some depth, is perhaps the most important activity to carefully control.

## HOUSE RULE - CONSEQUENCE

The column to the right of the house rules is CONSEQUENCE. If the rule is broken you need to state what happens, according to the child's age. If this is your first attempt to discipline your children systematically, then perhaps you should start gradually with just a few clear rules, so each child can learn without any stress. When these rules have become manageable, increase the rules. We cannot impose, too much, too quickly as we do not want to cause anxiety in our children. Just the opposite. The aim of the house rules is clarity, good habits and less family stress. You know your own child's capability. The following is a sample:

| HOUSE RULE | RULE BROKEN |
|---|---|
| Bed time is 8 PM. (TIME) | Reduce the time 15 - 30 minutes earlier |
| Sweep Garage (CHORE) | Empty dishwasher for three days |
| Family Story Telling (ACTIVITY) | Read & write report on one chapter in Sathya Sai Speaks |

## HOUSE RULES MEETING

After you complete your house rules worksheet, call a meeting with the children. Explain what the rules are, engage them in the process by asking them for any suggestions or questions or clarification. Consider their input but don't forget they generally will not want these rules, especially if they are a bit older. State clearly the consequence of breaking each rule. Have the consequence match the rule; don't keep changing them. Consistency is the key.

After you have the discussion with the children, (which should be a good two-way conversation) each of the members need to <u>sign</u> these house rules. Emphasize they are making a statement of commitment. Then photocopy the rules and paste them around the house. When a rule is broken, simply say, "The rule was broken, go read the consequence on the House Rules sheet". Parents, this is the end of the conversation. You do not engage in a renewed discussion of this house rule or any other rule every time one is broken. That was the purpose of the house rules meeting. Opening them to reinterpretation will wreck the entire process and defeat the purpose of this system. The rules are not open for discussion on what is acceptable or what is not, every time they want to do something. This teaches discipline, self-control and respect for social contracts. Your children learn the rules and what happens when they are broken. As in society's law, there is no scope for changing, rearranging or explaining. Once they are agreed upon consider the House Rules to be set in cement.

Swami has ashram rules. Is there any discussion on the part of the ashram officials? Never. There is a place to line up, and a time to line up. Children are not permitted to sit in the front row, children are not allowed to stay during darshan if they cry. Silence is maintained in darshan. Men and women sit separately. Appropriate dress is required. Cameras are not allowed. There is no grabbing at Swami's feet. Certain purses are not allowed for women. No standing during darshan. No calling out to Swami. Only vegetarian food is served. No smoking. No alcohol. Should I go on with the rules? Once clear, the rules should become aids for daily living. If they don't like your rules have them look at Swami's rules.

Within a matter of weeks after instituting this system you will find that life is easier. The children will quickly learn what is acceptable and what is not, and they will get the message. Have patience, it will work if you are firm and loving, as Swami is with us.

Start the written house rules at age two or three. Make house rules according to their age, and post them. Even though they cannot read the rules, you or their older siblings can read for them. When they break a rule, take them over to the work sheet pasted on the wall and read the rule and the consequence of breaking it. Consequences need to be small, for the tiny tots, like them, -- short time out's, no sweets etc., again determined by you and your spouse.

Remember, you are establishing a behaviour pattern and you are programming their subconscious. You're building positive habits. If you are working with newborn children, talk to them constantly about Swami's teachings. Do it with love in your tone and behaviour. This sets the stage for an easier time when they are older.

## MORE ON DISCIPLINE

There are two types of Discipline: **Active and Passive Discipline**.

Active discipline involves performing or doing something. This kind of discipline requires some actions such as service, chores etc. Passive discipline is a restriction of activities, such as no more of this or that. Swami uses

151

both types of discipline in his Ashram.

**ACTIVE DISCIPLINE** **teaches children to be more responsible for their actions.**

EXTRA CHORES: Laundry, Ironing, Cleaning, Cooking etc.,.

EXTRA SERVICE PROJECT: For Family Members or Community

EXTRA STUDY: Book Report, Writing Numbers Alphabet, Maths, Swami's Teachings

**PASSIVE DISCIPLINE** **teaches children to think of the consequences of their behaviour before they take action.**

RESTRICT THEIR ACTIVITIES: Television, Friends, Sweets, Car, Movies, Telephone, Outings, etc.

RESTRICT THEIR ACTIONS: To a chair, room or house.

| THOUGHT | WORD | DEED | CONSEQUENCE |
|---------|------|------|-------------|
| PASSIVE | ACTIVE | ACTIVE | PASSIVE |
| KNOWLEDGE | EXPERIENCE | EXPERIENCE | KNOWLEDGE |

<u>Passive Discipline</u> is restricting the child from some pleasure. They lose a privilege. It is restricting their activities. This gives them the time to think about what they did, and this engages their thought in the consequences of their actions. Consequence in this sense becomes the knowledge gained from our actions.

<u>Active Discipline</u> is not restricting the child but rather challenges the child to do more work, extra chores, service or study. This teaches the child that more effort is needed on

their part to complete an act. If they are lazy, selfish and not interested in completing the job to satisfy the parents, this active discipline engages the word and deed, the promise and performance part of our act. Combining these two types of discipline will strengthen the knowledge and experiential part of their nature.

Most parents use the passive discipline, restricting some activity, but to achieve a balance it is necessary to use active discipline as well. This takes more effort on your part because you will need to monitor their work. But soon they will get the message and learn to do the jobs well.

I remember when I would say to my mom, "I'm bored!" She would say, "Good, here's a bucket, clean the windows." (I soon learned not to complain of boredom, anymore.)

Another method of discipline you can use is to teach them Sai's teachings. Swami has so many beautiful teachings on children's behaviour. If they disobey, you can have them find the rule or teaching that they have broken in the Sathya Sai Speaks Editions. Or, for younger children, you can gather His quotes (on keeping bad company, movies, television, wasting money, fighting, anger etc., etc.) onto a paper. Ask them to locate the exact quote that they broke and write it so many times. This will both teach them the quote and program their subconscious.

One day when we were in Brindavan, Swami stopped going near the boy students. He did not invite them into His house. This "cold shoulder" went on for a month. One of the teachers said to Swami, "Two boys did something wrong; why Swami are you punishing all the students?"

Swami replied, *"Two are getting punished and the rest are learning not to do the same thing."*

In case you are not familiar with Swami's Brindavan trips let me explain the severity of this punishment. Swami is rarely at Brindavan and usually remains only during March and May. When Swami comes to this campus He allows the students to come into His house every evening where He talks with them. Sometimes Bhagavan gives a discourse or they sing bhajans while He sits in a Jhoola at the head of the parlour. To the boys this is the most precious time on earth. Time stands still for them. There is nothing but the Bliss of the Lord shining on them. It is a private "family time," in essence, a group interview every night, and sometimes in the morning as well. So when Swami took this away and avoided them in Darshan, it was indeed a very, very severe punishment.

I thought about this and wondered how I could have used this example with our children? I recalled how many times the children would fight, and come yelling. I never knew who caused the fight because I did not see it, and invariably they would blame one another. I had to be a policeman, detective, jury and judge without any facts! I hardly ever came to know the real truth. Even today, my children will say, "Remember when the cake got smashed, and you punished Craig? It was really me!"

Well, dear parents, here is your solution. When there is a problem or a fight, and you do not have a clue who was at fault, punish them all! Brilliant Swami! They will all soon learn that if any of them fight they will all get punished. This is positive peer pressure.

## CONTRACT

This is a method of discipline for children that is not covered in the House Rules, and can be especially helpful with the older children.

### A SAMPLE "CONTRACT".

**JANE/JOHN** *(CHILD'S NAME)* **AGREES TO DO** - *(word)*

*STATE OBLIGATION* - *(thought & deed)*

**IF BROKEN, THE CONSEQUENCE WILL BE** *(STATE DISCIPLINE* - *(consequence)*

SIGNED:     PARENTS     CHILD

---

To give you an example. **John will agree to be home tonight with the car at 11:00 PM. If late, he will loose car privileges for the next two week-ends.**

**Signed   Mom or Dad_____ John_____**

This contract covers all the steps of thought, word, deed and consequence, and teaches all the values. It is a complete learning experience for the child.

Let's say that John broke the contract and did not come home till 1 AM. You don't need to sit and wait to talk with him at 1 AM. No, you have a contract with his name on it. The next morning you simply produce the contract, have him read it because he must have forgotten what he signed. End of conversation. No wrenching, arguments. No induced guilt. Simply honor the agreement.

Take this contract form, make copies and keep them handy. Use a contract for everything that is not on the house rules list. Example, Contract: Mary will rake the leaves after school today, if not she cannot go to the Arts and Craft Fair on Saturday.

## BECOME A PERFECT MIRROR

Another hint I learned from Swami was this. When we don't listen to Swami, He doesn't talk to us. When your children don't listen to you, don't listen to them. If they don't do as you request; don't give them what they request. Become a mirror reflecting their behavior as Swami does to us.

We, as parents often talk so much that our children simply tune us out. In today's remote controlled world, just push "mute" and off goes the sound of parents!

Because they live in noise, they may respond more to actions. Well, ignore them. Stay silent. Behave in a way that engages their passive side (or inner side), the thinking part of their nature.

Also if a child is behaving in a negative manner, don't give any energy to the negative behaviour. For example, a child wants a cookie from the pantry when dinner is going to be served in 15 minutes. You explain why they cannot have it and the child throws a yelling fit and rolls on the floor. If they continue to yell remove yourself from the room or put the child in his/her room. If they are going to act in this manner, you do not need to be subjected to it. The point is not to add any energy to negative behavior, but to only reinforce the positive. If the child gets angry, send him/her to their room, out of your sight. If they have no audience, they soon stop performing.

## PARENT HOUSE RULES

Swami says, *"In some houses, parents quarrel in front of their children, which is an unhealthy practice. If there is any difference of opinion among parents, they should resolve it in the absence of their children. Children cannot concentrate on their studies if they are disturbed by family problems. So parents should never discuss problems in front of their children."* Sathya Sai Newsletter Summer 1999 pg. 33

Here are a few Parent Rules.

* Never fight with your spouse in front of the child

* Never disagree in front of the child

* Maintain consistency

* Never give permission unless spouse is consulted (whenever possible)

* Agree on "House Rules" and "Methods of Discipline" with spouse and with children

* Listen with love and total attention (<u>stop</u> what you are doing & look at them)

* Speech needs to be:

**Remember:**

| Clear | Decisive | Loving | Understood |
|-------|----------|--------|------------|
| *thought* | *word* | *deed* | *consequence* |

Swami says, *"The spoken word, though it may be short and appears to be only a sound, has in it the power of the atom bomb. Words can confer strength; they can drain it off. Words can gain friends; they can turn them into enemies, they can elevate or lower the individual."* SSS #11 pg. 143-144

# HOUSE RULES WORKSHEET

**NAME** _____

| Activity | Mon. | Tue. | Wed. | Thu. | Fri. | Sat. | Sun. | Consequence |
|---|---|---|---|---|---|---|---|---|
| Prayer | | | | | | | | |
| Bed Time A.M. | | | | | | | | |
| P.M. | | | | | | | | |
| Homework | | | | | | | | |
| Quiet Time | | | | | | | | |
| Chores | | | | | | | | |
| | | | | | | | | |
| Family Activities | | | | | | | | |
| | | | | | | | | |
| Individual Activities | | | | | | | | |
| | | | | | | | | |
| Television | | | | | | | | |
| | | | | | | | | |
| | | | | | | | | |
| Allowance | | | | | | | | |

## SAMPLE CONTRACT "CLAUSE"

_____

(Child's Name)

**AGREES TO....**

_____

_____

(State Obligation)

**IF BROKEN, THE CONSEQUENCE WILL BE :**

_____

_____

(State Discipline)

Signature

_____        _____

(Mom or Dad)                    (Child)

_____

Date

# CHAPTER 13

# TELEVISION OR TELEPOISON

*TV rots the senses in the head!*
*It kills the imagination dead!*
*It clogs and clutters up the mind!*
*It makes a child so dull and blind.*
*He can no longer understand a fantasy.*
*A fairyland!*
*His brain becomes as soft as cheese!*
*His powers of thinking rust and freeze!*

An excerpt from *Charlie and the Chocolate Factory*,By Roald Dahl., 1964

Outside influence comes from persons, places and things. This too is a vast subject that has many different aspects. The first of these subjects and the most damaging in my generation has been the irresponsible use and programming of the television. The present generation has the Computer, Internet and Video Games to add to the perplexity of parenting.

We all feared, in the sixties, that the Atomic Bomb would destroy our world. Unaware, blindly unaware we slept, only to awaken two generations later to discover that television, movies, and internet, in their ultra-sophisticated style, were shrewdly destroying the home of our morality.

When I was young, we lived one block from the Catholic Church, and most of my activities centered around the church. I attended daily mass, school, sports after school, and music lessons from the nuns. It was so peaceful compared to our present day lifestyle.

The community was small, even though it was in the countryside of St. Louis. My parents were raised in this same community. Their parents, and their brothers and sisters lived near our home. School friends of my parents, married each other, and many of their children were my friends. The community formed an extended family of shared values. Mom and dad basically had a controlled environment in which to raise us. No one in this environment disagreed with their lifestyle, morality or religious beliefs. They were the primary influence in our home, and their teaching was rarely challenged by the culture at large.

It is the same in Swami's Schools. He too has a controlled environment for the students. This is the very best of worlds for a child because it avoids the confusing clamour of divergent and conflicting moral values and beliefs. Swami tells the students when they go home to be careful and practise what He taught them. He tells them that their mothers will have them sleeping late and stuffing their mouths with food in front of the television.

Swami said, *"As long as the children are in our ashram, they behave well, and do everything well. The moment they go home for a short holiday to their parents, the children change their behaviour. The fault is not with children. The parents are responsible, because of the so called love that parents normally exclaim."* Swami's talks to the Students

Swami knows the enormous influence the students face from the contemporary culture. He knows that until the child is spiritually mature these outside influences can undermine all the work that He has inspired. This is the dilemma that we parents face. We are no longer the primary influence even within our own homes! The outside world creeps electronically into our living room and into our childrens' bedrooms to insinuate the advertising industry's value system into our family's values. Although we don't have a controlled environment as did our parents, we can and must strive to make it as controlled as possible.

Let's examine the subject of the largest, most powerful, and most insidious influence in our homes: TELEVISION!

Sai says, *"From the moment television made its appearance, the mind of man has been polluted. Before the advent of television, men's minds were not so much polluted. Acts of violence were not so rampant previously."* SS January 15, 1996

The above statement is **profound**. Just think about the reality of this statement. He says that television is largely responsible for "mind pollution". Why do we allow this pollution to continue? Why do we contaminate our own minds and those of <u>our children</u> with this instrument of so-called pleasure? This invention creates chaotic, violent, untrue images in our mind which most times are anything but pleasing to our emotions. How ignorant and irresponsible we are with the good advice that we receive from Swami! We simply bury our head in the sand, and don't take the time to think through and really understand what He is telling us. The entertainment that the "tube" gives our children is polluting their minds, their emotions and their vulnerable hearts. We would not feed our children spoiled food. Then why are we feeding them rotten, frightening dreadful food for their minds and souls?

Sai says, *"Young people should realize that the root cause of all their bad thoughts and bad actions is the food they consume. The nature of the food determines the state of the mind. Food does not mean merely what is eaten, but includes all that is received through the senses and stored in the mind."* SS January 15, 1996

We all know that the pure Satwic food that Sai has instructed us to eat, also includes the food we feed to all our senses, seeing, hearing, tasting and smelling. The body is a large video camera which records all the events that we view on the film of our memory.

He says, *"Hear no evil, hear what is good,*

*See no evil, see what is good,*

*Think no evil, think what is good,*

*Do no evil, do what is good."*

Our behaviour evolves from our unconscious programming. It is more difficult to think and do good, when we have been programmed with visual and audio negativity. It stands to reason that the tape of a child's mind is recording ALL THE TIME, and it is sometimes NOT ERASABLE! This is the part that is frightening, and contributing to the present day horror that is being exhibited in the behaviour of mass shootings of both adults and children, the violence and crime witnessed daily on the screens, with no virtual accountability for the movie and television producers. Instead they are rewarded with wealth.

We see shootings, blood baths, murders, profanity, pornography, satanism, violence, screaming, fighting, and arguing on the television, movies, internet, and video games. In a recent interview, movie producers were asked, "Why are the movies more violent today and what is the need for so much foul language?" They replied, "The people are now desensitized, and in order to get their attention, we need to use these methods." It seems that "shock therapy" is needed to attract our attention. Perhaps our senses are numb with media blasting. Greed certainly explains the nature of the beast that influences the producers in every avenue of the multimedia.

Sai says, *"There is now what is called 'Star TV'. It is doing great harm to human life. The temporary satisfaction given by it is followed by lasting damage. It is like a sword coated with honey. As you lick the honey, the sword will cut your tongue."* SS Discourse January 15, 1996

I see children viewing scenes of horror that I cannot watch myself, having protected my senses for so many years. But many children nowadays are so saturated with this daily violence, this garbage, that they cannot distinguish between what is good or bad for them. Their powers of discrimination have not developed and they believe with a *certainty* that this show or that movie will not have a negative effect on them. But we are the parents and we know better. We must be loving but FIRM.

I was frequently accused of being "old fashioned". My reply: "If old fashioned means good moral values, then yes, I am old fashioned." We cannot be intimidated by their opinions.. We are strong; we have the Atmic strength of Sai flowing within us, each and every one of us.

Is it any wonder that children, with their regular diets of television, MTV, films, internet craziness and video killing games, are fearful and restless. And is it any wonder that when they reach their teens they sometimes seek to escape this world of fear, with drugs or alcohol or more violence? There is little peace in their young minds because of the terror they have fed upon for years.

Teenagers believe it's "cool" to be able to view the grossest programs and films. Why have we as a nation generally lost interest in viewing pleasant and good, beautiful, majestic, loving and inspiring art? Why are we being subjected instantly and constantly to so many evils in the world? Why is it we so rarely hear the good? My mother-in-law would have said, "Satan is running loose!". Swami's explanation is that this is the Kali Yuga.

Years ago, local gossip was more or less the extent of "evil". Today, every tragedy that happens locally, nationally or internationally, we soak up on the spot with the evening news. Then at bedtime we toss and turn, the mind churning with the thousands of pictures that have assaulted us, most of them images that we have not had time to digest. These scenes run through our consciousness seeking understanding.

Sai says, *"Concentration on the television affects one's view of the world. The scenes, thoughts and actions displayed on the TV set fill the mind of the viewers. Unknowingly, agitations and ill-feelings, enter their minds. In due course they take root and grow in the minds."* SS Discourse January 15, 1996

We cannot trust even the Disney films. I recall a little 8-year old boy saying, "I don't want to see that <u>Pocahontas</u> movie, there is too much kissing stuff in it." Robert and I made a point of viewing this movie after his statement. Sure enough the child of eight was correct.. It's a very sensuous, animated children's film. How many millions of hearts and minds in our nation have been programmed w ith this? There is no eraser.

Sai says, *"Television or Telepoison? Do not read trash or see foul films."*

Once at a friend's house, I observed a little two year old playing in a room with the cartoons playing on the television set. He was not watching them. Suddenly, I heard someone saying, "I hate my daddy, I hate my daddy, I hate my daddy." "Where is this coming from?" I thought. I went into the family room and saw this cartoon character repeatedly yelling and screaming this statement. What a terrible message to be driving into the depths of innocent children's minds.

Does this affect the children? One year later, we returned to that house. This same child was being reprimanded by his father. The child screamed, "I hate my daddy", over and over again. The father wondered where the child had learned this; definitely not from his parents. The father felt really unhappy that he had to correct his little boy. The child was not aware of what he was saying, and he didn't understand its true meaning. It served as a clear example to me of the direct correlation between television and the child's words. No one in the family had made this kind of statement. Let me assure you, it came from that "innocent" cartoon. This message was programmed into that young mind twelve months earlier.

Sai says, *"Films and television have totally demoralized the people. People have become completely oblivious to Divinity within them."* SS Discourse January 15, 1996

Never trust anyone's opinion of what is good for your child to view. How many times do you hear an adult say this is a "great film" only to find that it is not? We would occasionally go to the movies on the advice of someone; because of our sensitivity, we often had to walk out, because we found it objectionable!

Sai Baba says, *"Parents must examine every story or account that you place before the children from the point of view of individual faith and social harmony. Does this lead the child to a better more harmonious, a more God-oriented life? That is the question you should ask yourself."* SSS #9 pg. 1

My generation was the first to raise children with television. I could not understand why my parenting skills (which I largely assimilated from my mom and dad) were not working so well? Why were the children not conforming as I did? At the time, we didn't suspect that television was the culprit. It was too new and its long-term imput was yet unknown. There was no negative data about this "miracle" of inventions. Imagine bringing pictures from the wide world into your own home! Imagine having movies, news, vaudeville, theatre, sports, all in your own living room! Who would ever question this phenomenon except the one who is Wisdom itself, Sri Sathya Sai. He knew it's impact on our soul. How often He warns us and we ignore Him. Sai, the Divine Parent, has problems with us, His adult children, as well!

Sai Baba says, *"For years you listen to Swami's discourses. How many have changed? How many have developed good qualities? Very few indeed. Women change yourself and help to change the men and the children."* SS Ladies Day Nov-Dec pg. 295

Years ago, psychologists would report that television was not harmful. I always wondered why manufacturers would spend millions of dollars on commercials to change our buying habits, if what we see on TV had no effect on us? How is it that it could influence our purchasing behaviour but not our moral behaviour? Is there a difference? We were assured that the violence that our children were viewing on the screen did not make their behaviour aggressive. This is simply a matter of common sense. Even today, rarely are the negative effects of television acknowledged by the marketing establishment. What has happened to common sense?

There is an insightful article by Dr. Susan Johnson, "TV and Our Children's Minds", that supports Sai Baba's teachings with scientific research on the negative influences of television. The following excerpts in this chapter will be from her paper.

She writes, "As a mother and a pediatrician who completed both a three-year residency in Pediatrics and a three-year subspeciality fellowship in Behavioural and Developmental Pediatrics, I started to wonder: 'What are we doing to our children's growth and learning potential by allowing them to watch television and videos as well as spend endless hours playing computer games?

"I practised seven years as the Physician Consultant at the School Health Centre in San Francisco, performing comprehensive assessments on children, ages 4-12, who were having learning and behavioural difficulties in school. I saw hundreds of children who were having difficulties paying attention, focusing on their work, and performing fine and gross motor tasks. Many of these children had a poor self-image and problems relating to adults and peers. As a pediatrician, I had always discouraged television viewing, because of the often violent nature of its content (especially cartoons) and because of all the commercials aimed at children. However, it wasn't until the birth of my own child, 6 years ago, that I came face to face with the real impact of television. It wasn't just the content, for I had carefully screened the programs my child watched. It was the change in my child's behaviour (his mood, his motor movements, his play) before, during and after watching TV that truly frightened me.

"Before watching TV, he would be outside in nature, content to look at bugs, make things with sticks and rocks, and play in the water and sand. He seemed at peace with himself, his body, and his environment. When watching TV, he was so unresponsive to me and to what was happening around him, that he seemed glued to the television set. When I turned off the TV he became anxious, nervous, and irritable and usually cried (or screamed) for the TV to be turned back on. His play was erratic, his movements impulsive and uncoordinated. His play lacked his own imaginative input. Instead of creating his own play themes, he was simply re-enacting what he had just seen on TV in a very repetitive, uncreative and stilted way.

"At age 3 ½ years, our son went on a plane trip to visit his cousins near Boston, and on the plane, was shown the movie "Mission Impossible." The movie was right above our son's head making it difficult to block out. Earphones had not been purchased, so the impact was only visual, but what an impact it had on our son. He had nightmares and fears about fires, explosions, and bloody hands for the next 6 months, and his play was profoundly changed. One of my colleagues told me I just had an overly sensitive child, and because I had not taken him to see a movie or let him watch much TV, he was not "used to it" and that was why he was so disturbed by the pictures he saw. All I could think was thank heaven he was not "used to it".

"Later that year, I assessed six different children from ages 8 - 11 years at the School Health Centre who all had similar difficulties with reading. They couldn't make a mental picture of letters or words. If I showed them a series of letters and asked them to identify one particular letter, they could do it. I wondered what happens to a developing child placed in front of a TV set if they are presented with visual and auditory stimuli at the same time. What is left for the brain to do? At least with reading a story or having a story read to them, the mind can create its own imaginative pictures.

"A question arose and I immediately called up my colleague and asked: "Could television itself be causing attention problems and learning difficulties in children?" My colleague laughed and said just about everyone watches TV - even my child does - and she doesn't have Attention Deficit Disorder or a learning disability. I thought to myself: "Are we spending enough time with our children and looking deeply enough into their development and soul to notice the often subtle changes that occur from spending hours in front of the TV set"? Maybe some children are more vulnerable to the effects of television because of a genetic predisposition or poor nutrition or a more chaotic home environment. I wondered about the loss of potential in all our children, because they are exposed to so much television and so many videos and computer games. What are the capacities we are losing or not even developing because of this TV habit? I then started to read, attend lectures, and ask a lot more questions.

"Television has been in existence for the past 80 years, though the broadcasting of entertainment shows didn't begin until the 1940's. In 1950, 10% of American house holds owned a TV set. By 1954, this percentage had increased to 50%, and by 1960, 80% of American households owned a television.

Since 1970, more than 98% of American households own a TV and currently 66% of households own three or more TV's. Television is on almost 7-hours per day in an average American home. Children of all ages, from preschool through adolescence, watch an average of 4 hours of TV per day (excluding time spent watching videos or playing computer games). A child spends more time watching TV than any other activity except sleeping, and by age 18 a child has spent more time in front of a TV than at school.

"There have been numerous articles looking at the content of television and how commercials influence children's (and adults') desires for certain foods or material goods (e.g., toys), and how violence seen on television (even in cartoons) leads to more aggressive behaviour in children (Fischer et. al. 1991, Singer 1989, Zuckerman 1985). Concerns have been raised about who is teaching our children and the developmental appropriateness of what is presented on TV to toddlers, children, and even adolescents. Miles Everett, Ph.D., in his book, *How Television Poisons Children's Minds*, points out that we don't allow our child to talk to strangers, yet through television we allow strangers into the minds and souls of our children everyday. These "strangers" (advertising agencies), whose motivations are often monetary, are creating the standards for what is "good" or developmentally appropriate for the developing brains of our children.

"More importantly, several investigators (Healy 1990, Pearce 1992, Buzzell 1998, Winn 1985) have drawn attention to the actual act of viewing television as even more insidious and potentially damaging to the brain of the developing child than the actual content of what's on TV. So what are we doing to our children's potential by allowing them to watch television?

**"Question: What is so harmful to the mind about watching television?**

"Watching television has been characterized as multi-level sensory deprivation that may be stunting the growth of our children's brains. Brain size has been shown to decrease 20-30% if a child is not touched, played with or talked to (Healy 1990). In addition when young animals were placed in an enclosed area where they could only watch other animals play, their brain growth decreased in proportion to the time spent inactively watching (Healy 1990). Television really only presents information to two senses: hearing and sight. In addition, the poor quality of reproduced sound presented to our hearing and flashing, colored, fluorescent over-stimulating images presented to our eyes cause problems in the development and proper function of these two critical sense organs (Poplawski 1998).

"To begin with, a child's visual acuity and full binocular (three-dimensional) vision are not fully developed until 4 years of age, and the picture produced on the television screen is an unfocused (made up of dots of light), two-dimensional image that restricts our field of vision to the TV screen itself. Images on TV are produced by a cathode ray gun that shoots electrons at phosphors (fluorescent substances) on the TV screen. The phosphors glow and this artificially produced pulsed light projects directly into our eyes and beyond, affecting the secretions of our neuro-endocrine system (Mander 1978). The actual image produced by dots of light is fuzzy and unfocused so that our eyes, and the eyes of our children, have to strain to make the image clear. Television, like any electrical appliance and like power lines, produces invisible waves of electromagnetism. Last June, a panel convened by the National Institute of Environmental Health Sciences decided there was enough evidence to consider these invisible waves (called electromagnetic fields or EMFs) as possible human carcinogens. In the article it was recommended that children sit at least 4 feet from TV and 18 inches from the computer screen (Gross 1999).

"Our visual system, "the ability to search out, scan, focus, and identify whatever comes in the visual field" (Buzzell 1998), is impaired by watching TV. These visual skills are also the ones that need to be developed for effective reading. Children watching TV do not dilate their pupils, show little to no movement of their eyes (i.e., stare at the screen), and lack the normal saccadic movements of the eyes ( a jumping from one point to the next) that is critical for reading. The lack of eye movement when watching television is a problem because reading requires the eyes to continually move from left to right across the page. The weakening of eye muscles from lack of use can't help but negatively impact the ability and effort required to read. In addition, our ability to focus and pay attention relies on this visual system. Pupil dilation, tracking and following are all part of the reticular activating system. The RAS is the gateway to the right and left hemispheres. It determines what we pay attention to and is related to the child's ability to concentrate and focus. The RAS is not operating well when a child watches television. A poorly integrated lower brain can't properly access the higher brain.

"In addition, the rapid-fire change of television images, which occurs every 5 to 6 seconds in many programs and 2 to 3 seconds in commercials (even less on MTV), does not give the higher thought brain a chance to even process the image. It reportedly takes the neocortex anywhere from 5 to 10 seconds to engage after a stimulus (Scheidler 1994). The neocortex is our higher brain, but also needs a greater processing time to become involved.

"Reading a book, walking in nature, or having a conversation with another human being, where one takes the time to ponder and think, are far more educational than watching TV. The television — and computer games — are replacing these invaluable experiences of human conversations, storytelling, reading books, playing "pretend", and exploring nature. Viewing television represents an endless, purposeless, physically unfulfilling activity for a child. Unlike eating until one is full or sleeping until one is no longer tired, watching television has no built-in endpoint. It makes a child want more and more without ever being satisfied (Buzzell 1998).

"Maybe the most critical argument against watching television is that it affects the three characteristics that distinguish us as human beings. In the first 3 years of life, a child learns to walk, to talk, and to think. Television keeps us sitting, leaves little room for meaningful conversations and seriously impairs our ability to think."

But haven't we been told that television is educational and entertaining? There are some worthwhile programs that are educational, but this is the exception not the rule. Entertaining, yes, but at what cost?

Swami says, *"Avoid films, for they may be advertised as very educative and inspiring. The producers in their greed for profit smuggle in low debasing scenes in order to please raw untrained minds."*

Dr. Johnson writes:

> **Question: What's wrong with using television as just entertainment?** I enjoy watching Disney films like Snow White.

"Television seems to have a profound effect on our feeling life and therefore, one could argue, on our soul. As human beings, we become detached from the real world by watching television. We sit in a comfortable chair, in a warm room, with plenty to eat and watch a show about people who are homeless, cold, and hungry. Our hearts go out to them, but we do nothing. One could argue that reading a book could promote the same sense of unreality without action. The phrases "turn off the TV" or "get your nose out of your book" and "go do something" have meaning. Nevertheless, while reading a book (that doesn't have a lot of pictures) the child's mind creates its own pictures and has time to think about them. These thoughts could actually lead to ideas that inspire a child or adult to action. TV does not give time for this higher level of thinking that inspires deeds."

Sai Baba says, *"To earn real respect, you should do what you say. First "Be", second "Do", and third "Tell". Without the first "Be" and the second "Do", you cannot merely "Tell".*

How often, in countless ways our Dear Swami has taught us the principle of doing good deeds. And now we are learning that television inhibits the "thinking that inspires deeds". Did you ever imagine that television had such an extensive influence on our children's development?

He says, *"People may wonder why one should do meditation and devotional songs. Those are good actions. They are all good actions meant to sanctify the time, but God is not interested in them. What is it that you should do to make God happy? You should involve your body in good deeds."* Discourse September 29, 1998

Dr. Johnson continues, "Television projects images that go directly into our emotional brain. It is said that the words we hear go into knowledge while the images we see go into our soul. Pictures that elicit emotion are processed by the limbic system and the right hemisphere of the neocortex. If no time is given to think about these emotional pictures, then the left hemisphere is not involved. Watching television often eliminates the part of our brain that can make sense of, analyze and rationalize what we are seeing.

"We don't forget what we see. The limbic brain is connected to our memory, and the pictures we see on TV are remembered — either consciously, unconsciously, or subconsciously. For example, it is almost impossible to create your own pictures of Snow White from reading a story if you have seen the movie. It is also true that often one is disappointed when one sees a movie after reading the book.

"The problem with television is that children get used to not using their imaginative thinking at all, and they don't exercise that part of the brain (the neocortex) that creates the pictures. Children are not reading enough, and we aren't reading or telling them enough stories to help their minds create pictures. Creating pictures is not just entertaining, but the foundation of our dreams and higher thoughts (intuitions, inspirations and imaginations)."

Sai says, *"Parents should foster in the children love for truth and righteousness and tell them stories about the lives of great men and women. In the olden times, the elders used to tell the young children all about the nation's heroes and saints. Where are such elders today?"* SS December 1996 pg. 335

Dr. Johnson reports, " Finally, the heart is now seen as an organ of perception that can respond to a stimulus and release a hormone-like substance that influences brain activity. This phenomenon is referred to as our heart intelligence (Pearce 1992). Interacting with human beings is essential for the development of this intelligence. When we stand face to face and look into another person's eyes, we meet soul to soul and we get a sense of who they really are (Soesman). We get a sense of whether they mean what they say - in other words, whether they are enthusiastic and passionate about their subject. We experience their non-verbal language such as how they move, the tone of their voice, and whether their gaze shifts around when they talk. This is how we learn to discern consistency between verbal and non-verbal cues and, therefore, truth."

Swami says, *"Truth implies more than the correct reporting of what was seen. It involves the coordination of thought, word, and deed, and the recognition of the Eternal Witness of all these. The Witness is the Self, a sport of the Omniself."* SS February 1985 pg. 37

The final excerpt from Dr. Johnsons article is alarming, as well as insightful. It concerns the apathy that exists regarding the lack of empathy towards our fellow-men.

"Television can't give us this intelligence of the heart. It can shock our emotions and we can cry, laugh or get angry, but these emotions are just reactions. When human beings speak on TV, children are often doing homework, playing games, and talking to friends while watching TV. These activities help save their visual system from the effects of TV, but the underlying message is **that you don't need to listen when another person speaks or comfort anyone if you hear crying.** If the heart, like the brain and probably the rest of our body, gives off electromagnetic waves (Pearce 1992, Tiller 1999), then there is a form of subtle energy that only can be experienced between human beings by relating to each other in the same physical space. This subtle energy can't be experienced by watching human beings on television. Just as we must use all our senses to construct higher level thoughts or pictures of an object, empathy and love for others does not develop from seeing human beings as objects on TV, but by actively relating, face to face, with each other." Susan R. Johnson, M.D., Assistant Clinical Professor of Pediatrics, Division of Behavioural and Developmental Pediatrics, UCSF/Stanford Health Care and Gradutate of San Francisco Waldorf Teacher Training Program of Rudolf Steiner College. This paper was presented at the Waldorf School of San Francisco on May 1, 1999.

Swami says, *"Buddha did penance for six years. He approached elders and listened to their teachings, but he could not get any benefit from them. Ultimately, he inquired within and found truth. He said that sacred vision (samyak drishti) leads to sacred feelings (samyak, bhaavam), which in turn leads to sacred speech (samyak vaak). Sacred speech leads to sacred action (samyak karma). Spiritual practice (sadhana) does not mean doing meditation or repeating the name of God (japa). Undertaking sacred actions is true spiritual activity. Human society is bound by action, undertake good actions."* Discourse given September 30, 1998

Buddha long ago arrived at this ultimate truth. Now, we have the scientific explanation of his words! To recapitulate the wisdom of Buddha and the scientific approach:

Sacred vision, (electromagnetic waves form a subtle energy from the heart when we meet soul to soul) leads to sacred feelings, (heart releases a hormone-like substance...heart intelligence) which turns to sacred speech (we get a sense whether they mean what they say) which leads to sacred action ("empathy and love for others does not develop from seeing human beings as objects on TV, but by actively relating, face to face, with each other.")

Swami says, *"Have good feelings in your heart, speak good words and do good actions. This is called, 'unity of heart, word and deed'. Understand that this is the purpose of human life."* Sathya Sai Newsletter USA, Fall 1999 pg. 7

The message is clear. Moms and dads, <u>turn off the television</u>! Ask your children, "what can we do instead of watching television?"

Make the activities home bound. Don't reduce television, and increase your driving load. Children need to learn to entertain themselves. If they don't know how, teach and encourage them by giving them activities that develop their thinking, imagination, and intuition. Cover the television with a scarf or table cloth and put Swami's picture on top! Or place a large picture of Sai Baba covering the television screen, it serves as a constant reminder to "mind the mind."

## OTHER IDEAS FOR DEVELOPING A

## NON-TELEVISION MIND SET:

* Create your favourite bhajan, or devotional song.

* Create a play with a value.

* Make up a story.

* Dress up as your favourite holy person.

* Have a quiz show.

* Talent show.

* Have a cooking contest.

* Sports outside for the family.

* Scavenger hunts inside during the cold months. Let them select a theme and hide items that represent the theme.

* Read good stories.

* Tell good stories.

One parent told me, they turned off the television. "No TV under any circumstances." I asked him, "What happened?" He answered, "At first it was difficult because there were issues, family issues that we had not dealt with for a long time, which surfaced. We no longer had television to use as an escape; now we had to confront our problems. But we did, and the children eventually learned that they were not going to watch television in our house. They soon became interested in finding other ways to entertain themselves. Our children are no longer interested in watching television. Having mercifully broken the habit, they learned to enjoy reading, playing, and talking with each other." But learning new behaviour and adjustment take time. Don't get anxious and expect too much, too soon.

When TV entered my household in the 1950's it was valued as a tool for entertainment and information. The television in those days had programs of a more wholesome nature, with spiritual content, good role models, talent shows, and quiz shows. The television industry censored the programs then, but today this self-discipline has long been tossed aside.

We must not ignore what is now proven. If you look at the studies and the dates in Dr. Johnson's article, you will observe most of this research has been done within this decade. Parents are fortunate to have this information.

I remember doing a small workshop with the young Sai adults. It was another wake up call for Robert and myself. We asked them, "What are the negative and positive effects of television?" They simply could not see the negative effects! When I asked them, "Why don't you see the negative effects?"

They replied, "We've been 'rug rats' (laid on the rug watching TV) since we were toddlers. We don't _know_ anything different!"

I then realized that they had no "before and after" experience to compare. My generation, when gone, will be the last to have a comparison between life with and without TV.

I remember as a child, the quiet evenings of sitting on the porch with my grandmother, mother, aunt and sisters, sitting and watching the sunset while they knitted, sewed, and talked. On a summer evening you could hear the crickets and smell the flowers. Dad, hoping to catch a breeze, would stretch out on the floor in front of the open door.

I remember the excitement we felt when treated to a drive in the country and an ice cream cone on a hot summer evening. It did not happen frequently but when it did, it was a moment to treasure. My play time consisted of using my imagination to create games for myself and my sisters and friends. I could spend hours alone playing dress-up, acting on the stage of make-believe, never realizing that this era was soon to pass.

Sai says, " *If television is used for teaching good things, it can serve a worthy purpose. But this is not the case. The younger generation is being ruined by undesirable films and television programs. Their minds are being poisoned. It is not a sign of parental love to let children be ruined in this manner. Even parents should avoid going to cinemas. All the crimes and violence we witness today are largely the result of the evil influence of films on young minds.*"

# CHAPTER 14

# GOOD "MIND MOVIES"

*"Due to advancements in the fields of science
and technology, human values are lost and
minds have become polluted. On one hand,
science has progressed; but on the other hand,
the sanctity of the senses has regressed. Man is
happy seeing the advancements of science and
technology, but he does not realize how far he
has moved away from divinity."*
Discourse September 29, 1998   Sai Baba

If your son or daughter falls from a tree and breaks his/her arm, you immediately take them to the doctor. But how do we repair the thoughts and feelings of a child who has fallen from the tree of life and has suffered a broken heart? Without the key how do we discover the cause that is locked in the vault of their mind?

In the physical world it is easier to see  the problem and discover both the cause and solution.  The mental and emotional "problem world" is not as recognizable. It is more subtle, and therefore more difficult to ascertain and correct in our child or teenager and even within ourselves. How do we uncover and heal what is hidden?

"MIND MOVIES" is the topic we are discussing. We mould the movies of our minds by the subject matter that we allow to be projected on our inner film.  Parents, we are creating content in the minds of our child. How do we search into this mileage of film, edit, cut, and slice out that troubled section of their mind that is problematic, when we haven't seen, known, nor comforted, the inner cry that we did not hear? We see only the negative behaviour, not the source or extent of the damage.

Sai Baba says, *"The good and bad that you see and experience are the results of your own thoughts."* SS May 1999 pg. 124

We take our money, gold and worthwhile possessions to the bank for protection. We protect them from outsiders. The same common sense can be applied to our children. We need to guard their minds, and their hearts, their inner wealth. We are the bank of protection against broken hearts.

From their birth we have been their guardians even though when they leave our home it is difficult to regulate them. By explaining to them the process of mind movies, we can help them to become their own guardians.

Sai Baba says, *"The senses exist and function in relation to the objective world. They produce desires, impulses, feelings, emotions, etc. which go collectively to form the mind. Based on the desires and impulses, the mind builds an image or picture of oneself which forms the ego. Thus the mind and the ego depend upon the senses for their existence. They feed continuously on the sensations produced by the senses."*

The newest invention of this communication age is the computer and internet. The same situation that we faced with that of television, using them with unknown effect, is presenting itself with the computer, internet, and video games. The invention is phenomenal. How could it be harmful? There is a growing voice of concern.

Sai Baba says, *"Ignorance is on the rise with the progress of Science. Truly speaking science has not matured. Man has become senseless. All the trials and tribulations faced in this world are due to the so-called development in science and technology. It is not technology but it is 'tricknology'. Do not become a slave to such technology. Uphold truth and righteousness. Cultivate love and experience divinity."* Divine Discourse October 15, 1999

I quote from an article called *"Do Computers Make Kids Smarter?"* by Leslie Bennetts.

"By the time my son was 3 years old, he was so obsessed with the computer in his preschool classroom that I decided to get him one at home. To my amazement, Nick's teacher was horrified. 'Don't do it!' he exclaimed. 'If you get Nicky a computer now, he'll become a hacker. He's very drawn to this, and he'll spend all his time on the computer instead of learning the things he's supposed to be leaning at this age - not just basic information, but social, physical, and interpersonal skills. Please, please hold off.'

'How long?' I asked timidly.'

'Wait as long as you can', the teacher said, and there wasn't even the glimmer of a smile on his face.

"Such stern advice was the last thing I expected to hear. The emphasis on technology has become so overwhelming that, like many American parents, I feared I was depriving my child of a crucial tool because I hadn't installed a computer in his room before he was out of diapers. In a lot of households, watching toddlers develop proficiency with a mouse has replaced the thrill of seeing them master their numbers and letters.

"The battle of the experts is on going. Don Tapscott, the author of *Growing Up Digital: The Rise of the Net Generation* (McGraw- Hill) says, "Children who have access to this new communications medium will learn more effectively than those who don't. When kids are on-line, they're reading, analyzing, evaluating, comparing their thoughts, telling their stories, collaborating, innovating. The Web is becoming the repository of all recorded knowledge."

"There is no doubt that the Web is a tremendous instrument for accessing knowledge but even Tapscott admits that if the computers are not used "Right", the consequences can be dismaying.

"Jane Healy, an educational psychologist and author of *Failure to Connect: How Computers Affect Our Children's Minds - for Better and Worse* (Simon & Schuster) says, "It is truly bizarre that parents and educators have so easily bought into the industry's hype that working with computers and software is going to make kids smarter and prepare them for the future. I have great belief in the ultimate potential of this technology, but I think it's being done all wrong.

"If the wrong software is used too much, it can reduce a child's creativity and imagination. It can also shorten a child's attention span. The child is paying attention not because he's managing his own brain, but because it is being managed for him by the software. When he gets off the computer and tries to solve a math problem, he's going to have to know how to do it himself, without someone seducing him through it.

"Children can have significant increase in IQ if they use developmental software, but if they use drill-and-practice software, they have significant losses in creativity," says Susan Haugland, a Southeast Missouri State University child development expert who evaluates computer programs.

"Theodore Roszak, the author of *The Cult of Information*" *A Neo-Luddite Treatise on High tech, Artificial Intelligence and the True Art of thinking* (University of California Press) says, 'Students feel that information is all you need and it comes out of a computer. The fact that there's a whole world of books in the library is vanishing. These kids are under the impression that because there are a lot of eye-popping effects on the computer, that's superior. But the World Wide Web is a mishmash of whatever anybody wants to put up there, and what they often get is misinformation and incomplete information.

'A kid with a pencil in her hand is ready to write, and a kid with a computer is ready to begin a learning curve that starts with booting up and virus checking and includes learning the interface, arranging the desktop, fussing with screen savers, searching for misplaced files, downloading, uploading, and deciphering error messages unless, of course, the teacher does all that for the student and creates the illusion that it's easy to do. What kids learn from using computers is how to use computers. That might be valuable for people looking for jobs, but in school that's not the highest priority. Teaching kids they need this machine to answer a question is distancing them from the art of thinking.' "

A on-line survey of 615 families by Digital Research, asked, "Do you spend time with or supervise your children while they are on the computer? The results were: 35% supervise, 55% spend time, 10% no." Family PC September 1999 pg. 62

The complexity of parenting is alarming. Supervision of homework has been a parental responsibility, but now add to your list of duties, learning a computer, software competence and internet censorship, etc., etc. In a day that is already overloaded with activities there is the additional task of supervising computers, internet and video games.

Sai says, *"Swami has nothing to do with internet. Not only now, even in future also. You should not indulge in such wrong activities. This 'disease' has its roots in cities and is spreading like wild fire into villages polluting the village environment."* Divine Discourse Dasara October 15, 1999

The Internet is uncensored and your child can walk down the internet highway into any vulgar room without your knowing. If you own a computer with internet access, place it in the middle of the family room, or someplace where it is exposed. Do not allow the child to use the computer in a locked room, or behind closed doors. This is the safest way to monitor what the child is doing. The curiosity of a child or teenager is natural but do we want our children to be exposed to all the scum in the world? The child will object, but you are the authority in your home. I would tell my children, "This is your mother and father's house, and as long as you stay in our house, no matter how old you become, you follow our house rules."

Swami says, *"Some may appear very pious through their words and deeds, but if you observe their behaviour, it would be demonic in reality. Do not have faith in such people and do not lose your purity."* SS April 1999 pg. 97

We wouldn't allow our children to enter unknown places nor talk with strangers who have no face, no name, and maybe no character, who could be satanic, mentally ill or criminally-minded. And now, your child or teenager can walk into any chat room and communicate with anyone while in your own home. It simply takes a few clicks on the mouse. How frightening to have this type of tool in the hands of our innovative offspring. It is imperative that you communicate your thoughts and feelings and why you will not allow them to use this network without your approval. We need to teach them discrimination, and it will take more effort on your part because you will need to be informed in order to teach them.

Sai says, *"Today man is wasting his youth by misusing his senses. He is seeing and listening to unsacred things and indulging in talking ill of others. In the early age, the five senses are like five delicacies. Your life will be sanctified, only when you offer them to God. Otherwise better to be deaf, dumb and blind! For what purpose are the eyes given to you? Is it to see anything and everything? No. Eyes are given in order to see God. The eye, which is not even an inch in size, is able to see the stars millions of miles away. Such a powerful and sacred eye is being used for seeing unholy things? Why don't you use your eyes for seeing the omnipresent God, the beautiful panorama of Nature and having the Darshan of holy men?"* SS May 1999 pg. 131

I have stressed the negative aspects of the computer and internet because they can be a dangerous tool in the hands of our children. We all know the positive aspects, using computers and the internet for educational and informative purposes. This type of usage is not creating the problem. I would be seriously inconvenienced without the use of my computer to write, to e-mail my friends, and to do research on the internet. I am an adult and I know Swami's code of conduct. I will not visit the internet sites that are "bad company". But your children are not adults, so we must protect them and teach them the power of good discrimination.

Another concern of parents is the video games. *"Childs Play"* written by Carolyn Jabs for the Family PC October 1999 Magazine says,

> "The debate about violent games has become so polarized that it's difficult for parents to find sensible, workable advice. And what expert guidelines we do get seem to be about generic kids, as though what makes sense for an 8 - year old should also apply to his 15 - year old brother. It's no wonder some parents react to violent games with a 'not in my house' policy and others adopt a 'what can I do?' shrug. Neither approach is helpful. It's impossible to insulate kids from

popular culture, yet parents who ignore the issue leave children without the moral equipment they need to keep the violence in games from infecting their thinking and behaviour.

"Parents must come to terms with violent games, because we want to nurture what's best in our children and assure their emotional health, despite a culture that is increasingly preoccupied with violent images.

"Psychologists still debate the effect of violence on mature players, but they're nearly **unanimous in their conclusion that young children can be damaged by exposure to violent media.** 'Actions we observe and learn at a young age create a baseline on which we take all future actions,' says Leonard Eron, Ph.D., a psychologist at the University of Michigan who has spent his career studying the effects of violent television. Whatever we put into a child has enormous consequences."

Swami says, *I keep telling the students often that the childhood of man is like a tender banana leaf. At this age, this 'banana leaf' is very pure, attractive and lively. This 'leaf' containing the delicacies of five senses (sound, touch, form, taste and smell) should be offered to God. But due to the impact of Kali Age, man is offering these five types of 'delicacies' to the six demons: anger, lust, greed, attachment, pride and jealousy. After the demons eat away the delicacies', spoiling the 'leaf' in the process, man is offering the leftover unsacred food to God in old age. Is it proper to offer to God the remains of the food eaten by the demons? If man cannot recognize the uniqueness of humanness, what is the use of taking the human birth?"* SS May 1999 pg. 131

We seem to have an obsession with violence in America. The blame game continues, each segment of our culture points the accusing finger at the other; meanwhile nothing changes. If they cannot find a cause then there is nothing to correct.

Swami wants us to see, hear and speak no evil, to protect our senses and keep them pure. How can you have purity in your heart when you're shooting others in a video game? I know some games seem more innocent because instead of shooting people, they focus on destroying obstacles. Nevertheless, you are still destroying what gets in your way. Understand if you play video games from a young tender age, you are programming your mind's movie to "take out" whatever gets in your way. In addition to violence, they are teaching *selfishness*. Where is the concern for others? You are destroying them. Most video games appeal to a primitive level of survival and self-interest.

Sai Baba says, *"Children have no respect for Parents. They are selfish, selfish, selfish. Ask your child? Where from did you come? How could you even exist if it were not for your parents? The children today think I - I - I. They have no fear of sin, no morality, no compassion, no gratitude."* SSS # 9 pg. 1

Where is the game that teaches us *virtue* and awards points for helping others, instead of points for killing pregnant women? Yes, that *is* a video game plot!

Many of our children from toddlers to teens cannot pass a video game arcade without clamouring to be allowed inside.

What is this obsession?  What is this thrill of killing others? Is this our standard for entertainment?  To reiterate, Dr. Eron said, "young children can be damaged by exposure to violent media!"  Our nation is simply not getting the message. How much additional proof do we need?  The tragedy of yet more violence in our society?

Swami says, *"Suppose you have pure 24 carat gold with you.  After some time, you add copper to it.  Later you add silver to it and then aluminum and brass.  When new metals are added to the gold, its true nature undergoes a change and it loses its value.  Today man also is undergoing such a change.  When he is a child, he is pure.  As he associates himself with others he acquires violence and non-violence, righteousness and unrighteousness, truth and untruth."* SS April 1999 pg. 97

In a recent Family PC on-line poll of 732 families, conducted by Digital Research, 31 percent of the parents who responded don't preview the games their children want to play.  In the following section you will find a list of the worst games, do not let your children play them until you watch the game and decide.

THE WORST GAMES

"Violence has always been central to computer and video games, says Brent de Waal, an avid gamer who researched kids and video gameplay at Simon Fraser University in Burnaby, British Columbia. That's probably because shooting and blowing things up is the quickest way to get a player's undivided attention, if you don't kill it, it kills you.

"Several factors make the current crop of violent games more damaging.  One is the first-person shooter point of view; games in which a player looks over the barrel of a weapon create an intense you-are-there experience. The games also have an astonishing, stomach-churning realism, which lets you see and hear the simulated agony of victims on screen. Finally, there's a loss of moral context. Some games no longer even make a pretense of good guy vs. bad guys, it's just shoot anything that moves.

"Lt. Col. Dave Grossman, the author of *On Killing: The Psychological Cost of Learning to Kill in War and Society* (Little, Brown, and Co.), says these features erode the innate human reluctance to hurt another person. He points out that the military had trouble getting soldiers to fire their weapons in combat, until they started to use training devices that resemble video games. 'Data on the effectiveness of simulators is overwhelming,' says Grossman. 'And we're letting kids use murder simulators.'

"Here's a short list of games many adults find disturbing:"

| | | |
|---|---|---|
| CARMAGEDDON | DUKE NUKEM 3D | POSTAL |
| DIABLO | HALF-LIFE | QUAKE |
| DOOM | KINGPIN | RESIDENT EVIL |

Source FAMILYPC Magazine October 1999 *"Childs Play"* by Carolyn Jabs

Swami has spoken to us many times on the issue of keeping good company.

He says, *"Tell me your company; I'll tell you what you are. You will change when you are with good people. Good company is necessary for a good child."*

For years we have identified His quotes with peer association for our children. Today, with the television, internet, video games etc., 'bad company' has augmented to include machines with a violent fear - driven message.

Recently, our beloved Sai has heightened and expanded our awareness by the following quote on "Bad Company."

Sai Baba says, *"Bad company does not mean the company of bad people alone. Even the bad thoughts constitute bad company. You should not only discard bad company, but give up bad thoughts also. One, however does not become a noble soul by just giving up bad company and bad thoughts; one has to join good company and also cultivate good thought."* SS May 1999 pg. 130

It is far easier to control their playmates and activities while the children are young but when they leave your domain as teens, most parents experience a sinking feeling. I know this feeling very well. The mind worries and dredges up every conceivable horror. This is the time that parents must trust in the devotion, duty and discipline that you have taught your children, and realize that Swami is protecting and helping them. Pray to Him and surround your child with His divine white light.

I have seen Swami protect my children in ways that I could never have done. Only God could intervene. We plant the seedling with love and support the plant with a rod of discipline till it grows to maturity and bears fruit......the fruit of listening to their own conscience and loving God.

Sai Baba says, *"Man today is proceeding on the wrong path. You need not follow anybody. You should follow your conscience, which is your master. Follow the Master; Face the devil; Fight to the end; Finish the game. Your duty is to follow the four F's. Since you respect and follow the words of those who have disharmony in their thought, word and deed, you tend to forget your Swami, your true Self. This situation is of your own making. Follow your conscience."* SS April 1999 pg. 97

# CHAPTER 15

# RESPECT AND REVERENCE

**R**espect is becoming neglected in our present culture. There is a lack of respect in our common everyday interactions with each other such as: politeness, kindness, manners, caring and sharing. I have had people for no apparent reason, screaming or passing me negative gestures while driving a car. I have had clerks in the market place snap at me when I asked a question, doctor's personnel never calling me back, voice mail unanswered, and crabby, rude remarks on the other end of the phone.....responses that were unsolicited.

Where is the decency or common courtesy of just respecting each other, instead of treating people in a less than human way? We are neglecting each other's humanness. Swami has told us that we have three natures, animal, human and divine, and many are acting like animals, shamefully sub-human. I suspect you too, have had these experiences.

The art of teaching our children to respect God, grandparents, elders, parents, people, property, and self is culturally vanishing. When I was young, children gave up their seat on the public bus to any standing adult. We stood-up in respect to elders or our teacher when they entered our class room. We opened the doors for adults, carried packages, served them tea or coffee, and did not interrupt their conversation with others. Talking back to our parents was unacceptable.

Sai says, *"Give up your seat to someone who is older or infirm or more deserving, that is service."* Seva A Flower at His Feet, Grace Mc Martin pg. 90

When I was a student, I thought these acts were seemingly worthless; but now I know they were designed to teach me respect for my elders which in turn gave me self-respect. During my childhood, this type of conduct was the social norm.

Swami says, *Modern youth even mock at such old people. It is the seed sown by those elders which has kept our ancient culture alive to this day. Only the women of the nation can revive and restore to its glory the ancient culture of our land."* SS December 1996 pg. 335

In my high school classroom, we sat erect with our feet on the floor, no crossing of knees. We walked the halls in a single file and kept silent. We wore uniforms and make-up was not allowed. We were being taught to transform ourselves into ladies of honour, manners and self-restraint. As a teenager, I thought that these rules were ridiculous. But when I married and the hard times arrived, these disciplines taught by the nuns, helped to prepare me for my role in life.

In school I learned self-control, along with the need for daily prayer.

We prayed at Mass before school; we prayed before each class; we prayed at 12 noon; we prayed before meals; we prayed in the chapel, and before all sporting events. These healthy habits created a behaviour which, at the time, I did not credit my teachers with its great benefits.

What did these rules teach me? To have a constant contact with God, discipline, and respect for rules. Compare this with today's students. How many give their seat to an adult on a crowed bus or room? Have you ever visited a school during their class-room-break? It's combat.

I sometimes hear, that today's morals are not different than those of the past. I'm told, "The only difference now, is our errors are exposed. That is why society appears to have less values." Let me assure you, that is not true.

Yes, immorality existed from the beginning of our world, but I believe to a lesser degree. In my youth it was less rampant and public .The reputation of others was not trashed as it is today, there is no respect for the privacy of others. In my childhood, society as a whole learned and exhibited more human values.

Swami says, *"Family reputation's important. We should not discuss our family problems with outsiders."* Swami's talks to Students

As Swami has said, before television man was more moral. To give an example: Once a boy about 11 years old, wrote one very vulgar word on the telephone post. The parents in the neighborhood gathered together and approached the boy's parents as a group. The parents disciplined their child, by keeping him inside for one month, and none of us were allowed to associate with him. His act was looked upon with severe disapproval by the neighbourhood parents. Compare that with today's standards. Bad language is common place in our movies. This same vulgar word is used profusely.

Swami's methods of teaching His students is comparable to what was taught in my school days. It was good. I know the culture has changed, and I also know that it is presumably impossible to create the world that we had in our childhood.

We cannot go back to the past, but we can improve on the present based upon Swami's teachings. THIS IS YOUR MISSION AS YOUNG ADULTS AND PARENTS. You do not have to accept the status quo. As a Sai Family you will need to inculcate Swami's values in your own lifestyle, be creative, start a new trend, and teach the children what is harmful in today's lifestyle. You will need to COMMUNICATE BIG TIME! You cannot put your children into a protective bag and isolate them from the world. They will need to go to school, work and live in society. They will be exposed to harmful influences. Therefore you will need to strengthen their conscience, more so than my parents did with me, because their values were then reinforced by the extended family, the school, and society at large. This is not true today. You are like a lone wolf howling in the darkness of the night.

When your children become adults, they may experiment with some things that are not good, but they will hear your voice inside saying that this is not good and for this reason, followed by Swami's teaching. They will eventually come to understand the Truth.

Sai says, *"Discrimination is the faculty that enables us to distinguish good from bad, and confers upon us the ability to decide when and how much importance is to be given to various aspects in a given situation. Discrimination is a component of wisdom. Without discrimination one cannot pursue the right path. It is a mark of sagacity to display discrimination in all our actions."* Sathya Sai Vahini pg. 167

Respect comes in three's: Respect for persons, places and things.

### *Respect for persons*:

Swami says, *"In order to lead a regular life, you must bring the following to your daily life. 1. Respect elders, mother is first God. 2. Follow elders, father is second God. 3. Follow the teacher, teacher is third God."* Swami's talks to the Students.

I see children sassing their parents. They show disrespect with no correction from their parents. They yell at them, call them names, interrupt, argue, criticize and generally do not want to help their parents. They call this generation, the "Me" generation. They are more interested in "ME" than others. There are many reasons for this, which I have addressed in the previous chapters. Outside influence, material emphasis, peer pressure, over-indulgence etc., etc.

The issue is not what caused this problem; as Swami says, "Past is past". But what can you do as parents to correct this disrespect? **Do not expect it!** If you want your child to respect you, then you must demand respect for yourself. When your child verbally or physically abuses you or others and you fail to correct it, then you too are not respecting yourself or others. When we have low self-esteem, we take abuse from others. Self-respect like self-love is taught by example.

Sai says, *"Self-respect leads to self-satisfaction, which will in turn lead to self-realization."* Dasara Divine Discourse October 15, 1999

People sometimes think that self-love is not required for giving love to others. Can you borrow a cup of milk from me if I do not have it? No. It is the same with love or respect. How can you give what you do not have?

Swami says, *"You must remember that the mother and the father are Divine and each of them is like God. You must put these sacred ideals into practice in your life. In India the most sacred things are the respect for one's mother and father who have not only given their blood in giving birth to us but also starved themselves on many occasions to give us what we need! If you respect your parents today, your children will respect you in the future."* Recapitulation of Sai, Grace Mc Martin pg. 382

The older generation is not appreciated. They seem to be pushed into the background as if they have no value, but in reality they have much value.

Grandparents are truly an asset to the family structure. Grandparents are a living testimony that with God in their life they overcame many obstacles and survived with their values enriched and unaltered. They are an example of hope for the children. Include them in your family life as much as possible. The children need their wisdom, love and support. Grandparents represent the extended family and its roots, traditions, and continuity. They will give your child a sense of belonging, a sense of identity in the world.

If you are the first child in your family to have a child and your parents are new grandparents, have *patience* with them. This is new to them. I found that after being a parent to my child for twenty years or more, depending on what age they left home, it was not easy to turn off the parenting mode and immediately slip into the grandparent mode which I might add, I did not know. It took some time to learn to stop telling my children what to do. The switch does not immediately turn off. We have to learn how to become a grandparent, the same as we have had to learn how to become a parent. My first child to marry had the most difficult time; I had to learn a new behaviour. You both are in "role reversals".

Your mom and dad have been parents for at least 20 years or more with that much more experience. They want to help you avoid the same mistakes; they feel they've learned better ways from their experience. But you want to seek your own identity, you want to do it your way. I know, and it's important to be responsible and mature in your judgment. But please respect them and listen to their advice, as you listen to your friends. Take all information under consideration, and then you and your spouse make your own decision. We grandparents and new parents, need to be patient and kind with each other because we are both . learning a new behaviour. Love and understanding are always the key.

I have two Swami stories about advice to grandparents. One friend said to Swami "I don't like the way my daughter is spiritually teaching my grandchildren." Swami replied,

"It's none of your business!" Another friend asked Swami, "What is the role of a grandparent?" Swami replied, "At age 50 start turning lose of your attachment, and by age 60, you only observe."

My mother's advice to me was, "Whatever you do, don't offer your children advice; only listen, love and support them." Unfortunately, she didn't tell me this until I had made many mistakes, but who knows? I may not have been ready to listen.

When I asked a grandparent in our workshop, "Are you smarter than your grandchildren?" I got a startling answer. **"No"**, they replied. I was shocked. Every time I asked this question at different workshops, I got the same reply. This reply was based upon worldly knowledge. The grandchildren are familiar with the newest technology, computers, internet, video games the latest clothes, vocal groups, movies etc., etc. They are smart, quick, and intelligent, this is true......but in worldly knowledge.

We grandparents, need to have a clear understanding about the difference between what the young people know and what we understand.

Swami tells us, *"Worldly knowledge is always changing, but Truth is permanent"*. This is wisdom that comes from experience. *We grandparents cannot confuse worldly knowledge with the wisdom that we have gained from a lifetime of learning.* Your grandchildren do not have your ability to understand the profundity of truth, right conduct, peace, non-violence and love, which only grows in the rich soil of living and suffering. It cannot come from technology, only from contact with the Atma in ourselves and each other. How can this wisdom compare with worldly knowledge?

In a workshop, I asked an 8-year old, "Do you think you are smarter than your younger brother?" "Yes," she replied without hesitation. I asked the teenager, "Do you think you are smarter than your 8-year old sister?" "Yes," again without hesitation. I asked again the University Student. "Do you think you are smarter than your teenage brother?" "Of Course", she replied. There is <u>no doubt</u> in their minds.

I say, "Your brother is 13 years old, and you are 22, so you are 9 years older. Is this correct?" "Yes." "Because you are older does that make you smarter?" "Yes" was the reply. " If this is true, and your mom and dad are, let's say about 45 years old, and you are 22, then that makes them 23 years older than you.......so I must assume that they are smarter, too? Right? Now, if we do the same comparison with your grandparents, who let's say are 65 years old, and you are 22, that makes them 43 years older than you. Certainly in 43 years they have learned something that you have not had the opportunity to learn as yet."

Case closed, grandparents!

Ask your parents for their advice, allow them to contribute. It makes them feel needed. Remember, you will need to ask them, because after reading this chapter, they are no longer giving advice unasked!.

Sai says, *"Today the children have no respect for the mother. Mothers have also little concern for the children. Who is responsible for this situation? The mothers are the root cause. It is because of the pampering of the children in all sorts of ways by the mothers that the children tend to go astray."* SSS # 9 pg. 2

Years ago, I thought spoiling children was a product of the affluent nations, but after I spoke with women from China, Russia, India, and third world nations, I came to the conclusion that this is a **world consciousness** problem. The women from these third world nations do not have the money to spend on their children but nevertheless, they are doing the same thing. They are spoiling them by performing their chores and softening their blows just as we do. The children are not taught responsibility for themselves nor are they serving their parents. The "Me" Generation is not just a dilemma of the wealthy nations in our world, it is a world-wide enigma.

Sai Baba says, *You will find at home pictures of God, kept in a special place for worship. In every home, however, there are living gods, whom the sages ask you to serve and worship. They are your parents. They gave you life. You owe your health and happiness to them. They love you, they serve you, they give you as much as they can and even more. Yes, they often take less food, so that you can have your fill. They try to save money through various means so that you can be at school, or live in a hostel, or attend a festival or go on a school tour. The sacred books want you to honour them and worship them.*

*"Let your mother be your God. Let your father be your God. That is the teaching. Yes, how else can you thank them? What else can you give, in return, other than your love and service? Think of all the care, all the love, all the pain, all the hunger and sleeplessness they underwent for your sake, and* still *undergo for your sake! Be kind, be soft and sweet to them. Do not be rude and raw. Try your best to make them happy; obey them, for they know much more than you, of the*

*world and its dangers. That is the way to worship them."*
Recapitulation of Sai, Grace Mc Martin  pg. 382

Swami speaks with such clarity. Whenever you need to renew your reason for teaching them respect, read the above quote to inspire yourself. You might also read this to your child.

## Respect for Places:

Places of worship, monuments, national flags, and personal property, all are being defamed. Driving down the streets  you see writings or paint spattered on walls, and buildings. You see it on buses, and many public institutions. The lack of respect for national, religious, and personal property is a  sign that we do not care about what belongs to others, nor our own character and its moral values.

We teach our children respect for places by starting with our own home. Jumping on the beds and furniture, writing on the walls, picking the flowers, eating food away from the kitchen and dining areas, walking on the carpet with muddy shoes, all these liberties if not corrected, will teach the child that disrespect and misuse of property is OK. What we teach by example in our home, usually and gradually carries over to the outside world.

I'll never forget, when we were living in Australia, we traveled on a family holiday to Canberra, the capital of Australia. Robert, myself, and our four children were touring, along with a dear friend and her son.  There was a large courtyard with a magnificent fountain where tourists threw coins. My friend and I were busy talking and not watching the children. All of a sudden, I saw all our 5 children standing in the fountain and collecting the money. I almost died. I

211

immediately brought this to my friends attention and asked, "What should we do?"

She took my arm and hooked it into hers. Strolling by the fountain, she said in a loud tone, "Whose rude children are those?" We sent Robert back to collect the little rascals after they put the coins back into the fountain!

Swami says, *Observe the rules laid down in the Scriptures, respect the culture of your land and bring honor to the land of your birth. Mother and mother country have to be revered equally, according to the scriptures. You honour the mother by obeying her and fulfilling her wishes; you honour the mother country by paying heed to the age-long traditions and hoary ideals that have stood the test of time. No one honours a renegade, He condemns himself by denying his country. Protect your mother tongue and mother land with all your energy."* Recapitulation of Sai, Grace Mc Martin pg. 384

## Respect for things:

We in America have a surplus of goods. Buying starts in families at birth and with the new mothers who are expecting a child. Mothers and fathers shop at a "baby supply warehouse" that is filled with infant merchandise. The market is so lucrative that the merchants need a warehouse to store and sell items without which the new parents cannot live: baby furniture, a rocking chair for the mother, a changing table, bathing table, infant car seat, infant stroller, infant carrying seat, bouncy swing, bouncy chairs, baby bassinet, baby monitor, bathtub chairs, buggy, high chair etc., etc., etc. Each family almost needs a warehouse to store the items, 'personally designed' for you and your child's comfort and convenience. We are drowning in a sea of stuff.

I remember when I was pregnant with Craig, we didn't have a baby crib. So a friend of the family made a baby crib out of tomato sticks. Four full length sticks at the corners, and shorter sticks for the middle spokes. There was a board in the bottom on which to place the mattress. The first time I walked into a baby warehouse store, I walked around in a daze.

Respect for things is taught in the home, from infancy on up, by teaching the child to care for their personal items: toys, clothes and room. I found that when a child becomes a teen-ager, they forget all that you taught them about tidiness. Sometimes, I couldn't even see their bedroom floor for the layered covering of clothes. I don't understand the complexity of sloppiness with teens, unless it's their method of rebellion. Fortunately, it is just a phase that passes.

When my children became teenagers and were desperately in search of their own identity, we would try a compromise on small decisions. During the week they could have a messy room, but on the week-end everything had to be cleaned and tidied. I simply closed their doors so I did not have to look at the mess.

Sai says, *"Laziness is rust and dust."* SS April 1999 pg. 99

Most of the time it is laziness that deters our children from wanting to pick up their toys, or clean their room. Swami does not allow disorder in his ashram. He speaks to us about cleanliness as Godliness. Teaching our child to care for their personal belongings is teaching them to respect things, a step in the direction of respecting all of nature.

Sai Baba says, *"Debt to parents, one's body, is derived from the flesh and blood of the mother. How much sacrifice is involved in giving birth to a child and rearing him with continuous care and love is beyond description. The food you eat, the clothes you wear, the life you lead are all the gift of your parents. It is one's primary duty to please one's parents. Only thus is the debt to the parents discharged. Nor is that all. The debt to the parents has to be repaid by acting properly and rendering service to society."* SS May 1990 pg. 113

# CHAPTER 16

# WOMEN SYMBOLIZE SACRIFICE

## DIVINE DISCOURSE

*Rama's divinity blossomed under Kausalya's loving
  care;
Lava and Kusa could become powerful and famous
  due to their noble and virtuous mother Sita,
The love and care of Jijabai made Shivaji a great warrior,
Fostered with the love of his mother Putlibai, Gandhi
  became a Mahatma.
Is there anyone in this world who can take care of you the
  way your mother does?
Amma (mother) is the first word that man picks up in life.
The first letter of the word 'Amma' also happens to
  be the first letter of the alphabet.*

(Telugu Poem)

EMBODIMENTS OF LOVE!*In this world
there are many types of relationships,
but none equals the relationship that exists
between the mother and the child.  It is because of this intimate
relationship with the mother that one's own country is called
motherland. Similarly, one's own language is called mother tongue.
Among the parents, first place is given to the mother, next comes the
father. Not only in day-to-today life, but also in the field of spirituality,
mothers and women are given the highest regard.  For example, when
we mention the names of Divine couples such as Sita Rama, Radha
Krishna, Lakshmi Narayana, etc., names of the Goddesses come first.
What is the inner significance of this?  Mother represents Nature,*

215

*which is the manifest aspect of Divinity. Similarly, the body and Atma, the creation and the Creator, are closely interrelated. The body cannot function without the Atma. The Atma cannot be experienced without the body.*

*The Bhagavad Gita refers to Swadharma and Paradharma. Swa refers to the Atma and Para to the body. But, today people are under the mistaken notion that Swadharma refers to the Dharma of one's own caste and community such as Brahmin, Kshatriya, Vaisya and Sudra. Swadharma is Atmadharma. The letter 'Sa' denotes Divinity. It also signifies the four stages such as Salokya (contemplation on God), Sameepya (nearness to God), Sarupya (identify with God) and Sayujya (merger with God). Today man performs all his activities having faith in the external world. All that is physical and external is temporary. Only the Atma is permanent and eternal. In fact, the Atma is the real mother. It is not proper on your part to forget this divine mother.*

### Mother is One's First God

*Mother is given the utmost importance in human life. There may be a wicked son, but not a wicked mother. It is because of the noble feelings of the mothers that sons become virtuous, intelligent, attain exalted positions and earn name and fame. The Vedas declare: Mathru Devo Bhava, Pithru Devo Bhava, Acharya Devo Bhava, Atithi Devo Bhava (worship the mother as God, the father as God, the preceptor as God and the guest as God). It is the mother who fosters you and nourishes you. It is she who knows your choices and preferences, and fulfills all your needs. So, you should be grateful to your mother always. Though you cannot see Rama, Krishna, Siva and Vishnu, you are worshipping them because you believe in scriptures and what the elders say. But, how is that you are forgetting your parents who are responsible for your progress in life? First and foremost, you should show gratitude to your parents, love them and* respect them. Your blood, your food, your head, your money are all the gifts of your parents. You do not receive these gifts directly from God. All that is related to God is only indirect experience. It is only the parents whom you can see directly and experience their love. So, consider your parents as God. God will be pleased and will manifest before you only when you love and respect your parents.

Children can understand the meanings of the word fox or dog only when they see their pictures. Similarly, it is only after seeing the parents that one can understand the love of the Divine Parents (Jagatmatha and Jagatpitha). This is what I tell you often — if you understand the 'I' principle in you, you will understand the 'I' in everybody. Vyashti (Individual) has emerged from Samashti (society), Samashti from Srushti (creation) and Srushti from Parameshti (Creator). Only when you understand the principle of creation, can you understand the Creator.

It is the mother who teaches you the sacred principles like love, compassion, forbearance, tolerance and sacrifice. Mother shows the father, father takes you to the preceptor and preceptor directs you to God. That is why among mother, father, preceptor and God, mother comes first.

### Woman is Embodiment of Virtues

When Hanuman went to Lanka in search of Mother Sita, he found her sitting surrounded by demons under a tree in Asokavana. Hanuman felt very sad seeing Sita being harassed by the demons. He went back to Rama and told Him, "Lord Rama, I have seen Mother Sita being harassed and frightened by demons pointing sharp words at her. She was shivering with fear like a parrot in a cage" (Telegu poem). On hearing this, Rama and Lakshmana immediately set out to Laanka with the army of Vanaras, fought a battle with Ravana and killed him. As per the command of Lord Rama, Hanuman went

217

to Sita and conveyed her the good news. Then he requested Sita to permit him to punish the demons surrounding her who had put her to great suffering. Sita said, "O Hanuman, it is the responsibility of the subjects to obey the commands of the king. Just as you obey the command of Lord Rama, these demons also had to obey the dictates of their kind. It is not their mistake. They acted according to the instructions of the king. So, it is rather unfair to punish these demons. In fact, I suffered not because of these demons, but because of separation from Sri Rama". So saying, she narrated the following story.

Once in a forest, a hunter, on being chased by a tiger, felt tired and climbed up a tree. There was a bear sitting on the top of the tree. The tiger was waiting under the tree as it could not climb up. It was very hungry, so it wanted to gobble up the hunter. It requested the bear to push the hunter down so that it could kill him and appease its hunger. The bear refused to do so, saying that the hunter was its guest and it was its moral duty to extend hospitality to guests. But, the tiger continued to wait under the tree. After some time, the bear started to doze. Noticing this, the tiger addressed the hunter, "O man, I am very hungry. It does not matter whether I eat you or the bear. I will go back once my hunger is satiated. The bear is dozing. So, push it down without delay. I will eat it and spare you." The man did not have the morality of even the bear. He thought he could escape from the clutches of the tiger by offering the bear as bait. So, he committed the ungrateful act of pushing the bear down. As luck would have it, the bear, as it was falling, caught hold of a branch, climbed up and saved itself from the tiger. Then the tiger said, "O bear, you should never believe the human beings. This hunter tried to harm you, though you were kind enough to give him shelter and protect him." But the bear said, "I have done my duty. Each one has to face the consequences of his own actions. I will not harm just because he tried to harm me".

218

Narrating this story, Sita said, "No doubt, these demons have put me to a lot of suffering without knowing what is truth and what is dharma. Being the consort of Lord Rama, I cannot stoop down to their level and seek revenge. I do not want to cause harm to anyone." Hanuman said, "O Mother, it is but natural that you, being the consort of Lord Rama, are broadminded and noble hearted. You are the embodiment of dharma. It is a mistake on my part to think that you would permit me to punish these helpless demons." Then Sita said, "Hanuman, not only me but all the women are endowed with the noble qualities like compassion and love."

There is a proverb in Telugu that the house mirrors the qualities of the housewife. The women, barring a few exceptions, never stray away from the path of truth and righteousness even in the face of adversity. When the mendicant stands at the doorstep stretching his hands for alms, the husband may possibly drive him away, but the housewife always comes forward to give alms. There may be dispute over property matters between the father and the son, but the mother always tries to calm down the son with good counsel. The mother will always pray for the welfare of the son wherever he may be. At times, she may be angry or have a difference of opinion, but such differences are only passing clouds. One should not disregard one's parents yielding to the vagaries of the mind.

### Easwaramma, the Divine Mother

Easwaramma, the mother of this physical body, was first christened as Namagiriamma at the time of birth. But after her marriage, Kondama Raju, the grandfather of this physical body, being a Jnani (one of wisdom) and blessed with a vision of the future, started calling her Easwaramma (mother of Easwara). He used to worship Venkavadhuta. His was a joint family. He had two sons. The elder son, Pedda Venkama Raju, was the father of this physical body. His younger son was Chinna Venkama Raju. Two sons of his deceased *brother, Subba Raju and Venkatrama Raju, also lived with him. One day, as there was some difference of opinion, it was decided to divide the property.*

At that time, this body was eight years old. Kondama Raju said he did not want any share in the property and told them to divide it among themselves. The four brothers requested Kondama Raju to spend the rest of his life staying with each one of them. But Kondama Raju said, "I do not want to stay with you, I do not expect anything from you. Whatever I have earned, distribute among yourselves. But give me one property, Sathya. (cheers) If He is with me, I do not want anything else." Then he asked me, if I was willing to stay with him. I readily agreed. Both of us were staying in a small room. I used to get up early in the morning, clean the vessels and cook food for both of us. After making the food ready, I used to run to Bukkapatnam to attend school. There the lunch bell would go at one o'clock. I would run back to Puttaparthi, serve him lunch, have it Myself and then rush to school for the afternoon session. I maintained punctuality both at school and at home. Kondama Raju, being the one with wisdom always craved for Me. One day, he called Pedda Venkama Raju by his side and told him to change his wife's name to Easwaramma. He told this because he felt the divine vibrations originating from within. His intention was to convey that she was the mother of Easwara, God Himself. (cheers) But, Pedda Venkama Raju was not aware of the inner meaning of this name. He implicitly obeyed the command of his father and changed the name of his wife to Easwaramma.

## Kondama Raju's Last Desire

The new Mandir was built before Kondama Raju left his mortal coil. He lived for 116 years. But even at that ripe old age his eyes and legs were in good condition. So, he used to walk from the old Mandir to the new Mandir every day, without a walking stick. I used to say, "Why do you walk the distance? There may be cows and buffaloes on the way. You can take the help of a walking stick at least." He would say that his legs were in perfect condition and that he did not need the help of a walking stick. He was an ardent devotee of Swami. He used to come to Me early in the morning at five o'clock. Seeing him coming at a distance, I used to cover Myself with a blanket pretending to be asleep. He would come slowly, lift the blanket, touch My feet and return. He used to come early in the morning because he did not want anyone to notice him touching My feet. He was a little apprehensive about what the villagers would think if they noticed a 116-year-old grandfather touching the feet of his grandson.

On a particular evening, I went to Puttaparthi to see him. At that time, he was sitting on a cot, deeply immersed in singing a ballad, which described Rama lamenting over the fainting of Lakshmana in the battlefield. He was very fond of this particular episode from the Ramayana. Rama lamented, "In this world I might find another mother like Kausalya, a wife like Sita, but definitely not a brother like Lakshmana." This is what he was singing to himself when I entered his room. I said, "O grandfather, what are you doing?" He exclaimed, "O Swami, You have come", and fell at My feet. He said, "Swami, I am fully aware that You are not an ordinary child, but Easwara Himself. You are born in our clan to redeem all of us. But, I pray that You fulfill a small desire of mine. Dasaratha did not have the good fortune of drinking water from Rama's divine hands at the time of his death. But Jatayu was fortunate enough to be the recipient of such an act of grace in his last moments. Swami, let me also have the good fortune of sipping water from Your divine hands when my end approaches." I promised that I would certainly fulfill his desire.

The following week, I went to see him again after visiting Subbamma's house. Kondama Raju came to know that I was coming to his house. Immediately, he called Easwaramma and told her, "I *am not going to live any longer. Having known that my end has approached, God is coming to shower His Grace on me." She responded in an innocent way saying, "Where is God? How do you know that He is coming?" Then Kondama Raju said, "O mad woman, still you are deluded by the feeling of a mother towards her son! Look there, God is coming." So saying he pointed as Me at I was entering his house. She too was aware of My Divinity, but she used to get carried away by her motherly affection towards Me. Similar was the case with Yashoda. Though she had seen all the fourteen worlds in Krishna's mouth, she thought it was a dream or an illusion.*

*Kondama Raju told Easwaramma that Swami did not take sweets. Right from birth till today, I have not touched sweets. What is the reason? If I were to take sweets, thousands of devotees would start bringing sweets for Me. I do not take fruits either. I do not even touch milk or curds. I lead a very simple life. I take only Ragi gruel and groundnut chutney. Kondama Raju also used to relish this food. He used to say, "Sathya, serve me whatever you eat." Early in the morning, I used to prepare tasteful Ragi gruel, groundnut chutney and some green leaves curry. The whole street was very fond of My cooking. Sometimes, on My return from Bukkapatnam, I used to find all those afflicted with fever make a beeline in front of the house waiting for Me. Kondama Raju would tell Me that they were all waiting to take the pepper Rasam from Me as it would give them relief. Immediately, I used to prepare pepper Rasam and distribute a glassful to each of them. They used to feel very happy and later on expressed their gratitude saying, "Swami, your pepper Rasam has given us great relief."*

*In those days, on festival days, such as Sankranti and Ugadi, etc., the dhobis and barbers used to come to the house for food. In the house, there was no one else other than Kondama Raju and Myself. So, I had to prepare food for many people. Easwaramma (Swami's* mother), *Venkamma and Parvathamma (Swami's sisters) used to prepare various delicious items including sweet puris in their respective homes on festival days. When they could prepare sweet puris, why not I also prepare and serve the grandfather? So, I also would prepare sweet puris and serve not only the grandfather, but also the washerman, the barber and others. On one such occasion, Pedda Venkama Raju (Swami's father) came to see us at lunch time. Kondama Raju invited him for lunch, as it was a festival day. Pedda Venkama Raju had his lunch with us and felt that the food items were very delicious. He went home and chided Easwaramma and Venkamma for not being able to make the items tasteful. He said, "Look at Sathya, what a fine cook he is! Why can't you prepare the food items the way Sathya does?" From the next day onwards, he started sending them to Me asking them to bring whatever food items I prepared. They would come and complain that it was because of My cooking that they were being blamed at home.*

*When I was nine years old, Seshama Raju, the elder brother of this body, decided to take Me with him to Kamalapur for studies. He felt that I was wasting My time staying with Kondama Raju. But, the grandfather objected to this, saying that I did not require any studies. But, things happened the way they were destined to happen.*

*After the construction of Prasanthi Nilayam, one day I went to see Kondama Raju. He asked Easwaramma to get a glass of water. He told her, "God has come to take me away. He made a promise that He would pour water into my mouth with His divine hands before I leave this body. He has come to fulfill His promise." Puzzled by Kondama Raju's request, Easwaramma said, "You are not suffering from any disease, you don't even have fever or a cold. What makes you think that your end has approached." Then Kondama Raju said, "Death occurs as per the will of God. Just as birth has no reason, death too has no reason. This is the Truth of truths." Easwaramma did not want to argue with him. According to his*

223

*wish, she brought a glassful water and gave it to him. He sat down on the floor and made Me sit on the cot. He kept his head on My knees and said, "Swami, please listen to my prayer." Easwaramma was watching all this. She wondered how is that he had so much love and regard for his young grandson. Kondama Raju said, "As You know, I was doing a small business to make both ends meet. Perhaps I may still have to pay a paisa or an anna to certain people. Please bless me so that I am not indebted to anyone in my death." I said, 'so shall it be' and started pouring water into his mouth. He breathed his last as he was drinking water. His desire was fulfilled. Before leaving his mortal coil, he told Easwaramma not to get deluded by body attachment. He said, "Bodily relationship is temporary, whereas Atmic relationship is permanent. So, give up body attachment and develop attachment to the Atma."*

### Three Wishes of Two Noble Mothers

*From that day onwards, Easwaramma never stayed at home; she started staying in Prasanthi Nilayam. Every day both in the morning and evening she used to come upstairs and talk to Swami. She also understood My Divinity very well. When I appeared in the form of Lord Shiva to her, she would ask, "What Swami? Why are you adorning the snakes around your neck?" I would act innocent, "Well, I don't have any snakes on Me." She would move away saying, "Look, there are some snakes inside." But later on not finding any snake inside, she would ask for forgiveness. Like this on many occasions, she had the experience of My Divinity. Similar was the case with Kausalya and Yashoda. Though they knew that their sons were Divine, they used to get carried away by their motherly affection towards them. Mothers are highly noble and virtuous. Their nobility cannot be described in words. It does not matter if you do not acquire worldly wealth, but you should try to win the wealth of your mother's grace. Only then your life will be sanctified.*

*Iswar Chandra Vidyasagar was a noble soul. He was born in a poor family. He was living with his aged mother. He used to feel very sad seeing his mother wearing old and torn saris. After he completed his studies, he took up a job and started earning some money. One day he sat by the side of his mother and said, "Mother, please tell me if you have any desires. Now that I have started earning money, I am in a position to fulfill them." She said, "Son, I don't have any desires. It is enough for me if you lead a noble life." After some time, he got a better job and started earning thousands of rupees. Then again, he asked his mother to tell him if she had any desires. She said she had three desires and could not live in peace unless and until they were fulfilled. "Ours is a small village and there are many children who are wasting their time without going to school. So, please construct a small school out of the money you have earned." As per the wish of his mother, Vidyasagar got a school constructed in his village. Then he asked his mother to express her second desire. "Our villagers are suffering for lack of medical facilities. There is nobody to take care of them when they are afflicted with fever, cough or cold. So, I want you to construct a small hospital." Vidyasagar built a hospital too. Then after some time, he asked his mother what her third wish was. She said, "The villagers are suffering due to lack of drinking water. They are being afflicted with various diseases as they are drinking polluted water." Immediately, he got a few wells dug and provided drinking water to the villagers.*

*As the days rolled by, Vidyasagar's name and fame spread far and wide. He was a good orator. His speeches were not based on bookish knowledge. He used to speak on matters of daily relevance. So, people in large numbers used to throng his meetings to listen to his speech. He was a very simple and humble man. One day he was going to a neighboring village to address a gathering. He boarded the train carrying a small suitcase. An I.A.S. officer, who was going to attend this meeting, was also travelling by the same train. He was carrying a small handbag with him. He had not seen Vidyasagar before. As soon as he got down from the train, he started calling out for a coolie. Seeing this, Vidyasagar went up to him and asked where his luggage was. The officer showed his handbag. Then Vidyasagar said, "Why do you misuse your money? Do you need a coolie to carry your handbag? Let me carry it for you." He took the bag from the officer and carried it. After reaching the destination, the officer asked Vidyasagar how much money he wanted for carrying the bag. Vidyasagar said, "I do not want your money, I did it only as an act of service." The officer proceeded to the meeting place where Vidyasagar was supposed to deliver his speech. He was stunned to see the same person who carried his bag giving a speech on the dais. What a humble person he was he thought to himself and felt ashamed of his behavior.*

*Ishwar Chandra Vidyasagar spent all his earnings to fulfill the desires of his mother. Easwaramma also had similar desires. Once she told Me, "Swami, our Puttaparthi is a small village, the children are forced to walk long distances to attend school. She said she had a piece of land behind her house. She wanted the school to be constructed there. Though it was a small school, the inaugural function was a grand affair, attended by many devotees. The next day, Easwaramma expressed her happiness over the inaugural function and said that she had one more desire. She wanted a hospital also to be built in the village. She said, "Swami, I don't want to put You to trouble. If You are troubled, the whole world will be unhappy. So, if it gives You happiness, please construct a small hospital." As per her wish, I got the hospital constructed. Bejawada Gopal Reddy, a highly reputed person in those days, was invited to inaugurate the hospital.*

*The inaugural function was a grand one, attended by thousands of people from the neighbouring villages. Easwaramma did not imagine that this would be such a grand affair. Next day, she came up to Me and said, "Swami, it does not matter even if I die now. I have no more worries, you have fulfilled my desires and mitigated the suffering of the villagers to a great extent." I said, if you have any more desires, ask Me now. She replied hesitantly that she had yet another small desire, "You know that the river Chithravathi is in spate during the rainy season. But, in summer it dries to a trickle and people do not have drinking water. So, please see that some wells are dug in this village." I told her that I would not stop with these small wells and I would provide drinking water to the entire Rayalaseema region. (cheers) Easwaramma said, "I don't know what Rayalaseema is. I am satisfied if our village is provided with drinking water."*

Once, on a Sivaratri day, after I had completed My discourse, the Lingas were ready to emerge from My mouth. I sat on the chair and was in severe pain. Seeing Me suffering, Easwaramma got up from the gathering, came up to Me and said, "Swami, why do You suffer like this? Come inside, come inside." I said I would not come inside. She cried and tried to persuade Me, but I did not budge an inch. Unable to see My suffering, she went inside. As soon as she left, Hiranyagarbha Linga emerged. All the devotees burst into thunderous applause. Listening to this, she came back, but by then the Linga had already emerged and I was showing it to the devotees. All the people got up to have a glimpse of the Linga. As a result, Easwaramma could not see it. Next day she pleaded with Me to show the Linga to her. I said I had given it to somebody. But she said, "Swami, I have not seen. I want to see." I told her that she would see in future anyway. She said, "I do not want to put You to inconvenience," and went away. She never put Me to trouble any time. Whenever she asked Me for something, she would come back and inquire if she had given any trouble. To all the devotees who came, she used to entreat them not to cause any inconvenience to Swami. She used to be very much worried whenever any minister *came to have My Darshan. The situation in those days was such that even a policeman with a red cap was enough to frighten the villagers. Easwaramma used to be very much afraid of the ministers thinking that they might cause some problem to Me. This was only the result of her sacred love for Me. That is the greatness of mother's love. That is why she could lead a life of fulfillment and peace. In order to propagate this sacred ideal, this day is being celebrated as Easwaramma Day. This is to emphasize that each one of you should make your mother happy. If your mother is happy, Swami is happy.*

### Sacrifice Everything for God

*Everybody should love and respect his parents. But, if any relation becomes an obstacle in your path to God, there is no harm in leaving him. Here is a small example. Mira was the wife of Maharaja of Chittor. She was always seated in Krishna's temple, forgetting herself while chanting his name. One day, Emperor Akbar came to the temple and offered a gold necklace to Lord Krishna. Mira accepted it and put it around Krishna's idol. Akbar was an enemy of Maharaja. When Maharaja came to know that Mira had accepted a necklace for Krishna from his enemy, Akbar, he became very furious. He took it as an insult and threw her out of the temple. Mira felt very sad. Crows start cawing at the cuckoo when it begins to sing, but that does not deter the cuckoo from its singing. The people of the world are like crows. They speak as they like. But the noble souls will not be affected by what others say. Mira was in a dilemma, whether to give up Krishna or her husband Maharaja. She resolved that she would not give up Krishna even at the cost of her life. Then she wrote a letter to Tulsidas seeking his advice in this regard. Tulsidas sent her a reply, "From the worldly point of view, you should respect your father, mother, preceptor and husband. But when it comes to God, everything else is secondary. God alone is important. Bharata left his mother Kaikeyi for the sake of Lord Rama. Prahlada gave up*

228

*his father, Hiranyakasipu, for the sake of Lord Narayana. Emperor Bali forsook his preceptor, Sukracharya, for the sake of God. So, there is nothing wrong in giving up your husband for the sake of Krishna." Taking the advice of Tulsidas, Mira left her husband. She sang, "O mind, go to the banks of the sacred rivers Ganga and Yamuna, the pure water of which cools and purifies the body." (Hindi song) These two stand for the primal nerves, Ida and Pingala, that converge at the center of two eyebrows. She started singing the praises of Krishna and proceeded towards Brindavan.*

*There are many such great devotees who sacrificed everything for the sake of God. Women symbolize sacrifice. The Vedas declare: Na Karmana, Na Prajaya, Dhanena Thyagenaike Amruthatwamanasu (immortality can be attained only through sacrifice; neither wealth nor progeny nor good deeds can confer it.) You can sacrifice anything for the sake of God. But, sacrifice should not be done with a selfish motive or for self-satisfaction.*

*The Bhagavad Gita says that a woman has seven qualities, whereas a man has only three. So, never look down upon women. They are most virtuous. They are the very embodiments of Nature. Some women may think that they would have enjoyed greater freedom had they been born as men. This is a wrong notion. In fact, women are more powerful than men. With all the sacred feelings in your heart, respect women and be respected. Respect your mother, obey her commands. Mother protects her children in many ways. Even after death, she comes back and helps you in various ways. Never disrespect your mother or disappoint her. Do not hurt her feelings. Try to satisfy her in all respects. Only then the seed of devotion will sprout in you. Everyone should follow the dictum, Mathru Devo Bhava in letter and spirit, and be a recipient of his mother's love.*

*From Bhagavan's Discourse at Sai Sruthi'*
*Kodaikanal on 6th May 1999.*

# CHAPTER 17

# SWEET SPEECH

C ommunication is the method we use to understand one another. The problem we have is how we code and decode what each other has said. We base our interpretation on our own programming, which is always anything but objective. Sometimes we think we understand what someone has said and when we question to confirm, we realize that we initially misunderstood.

We can seldom be too careful with our words. After talking with our child, it can be helpful if we ask them to feedback what we said. This simple step can prevent an error because immediately, you can rectify the statement. This is critical, especially in a heated exchange of words, or with instructions that a child must follow. Sometimes their thoughts are preoccupied and they are not completely focusing on what you are saying.

Listening is a major part of communication. When we listen to each other, we need to **stop** whatever we are presently doing, look the person in the eye, and concentrate on listening. Sometimes when my children would talk to me, I was cooking, or reading the paper or performing some task while trying to listen. This is not good for two reasons:

1. The person talking does not have your full attention and they know it.

2. You can easily misunderstand what was communicated.

Many teenagers or young adults complain that their parents are not listening to them. Perhaps "how they are listening," is also contributing to this predicament. Our youth are extremely sensitive; they need recognition during this labor to establish their own identity. Remember your own youth. Wasn't it sometimes traumatic? Give them your full attention, ask questions and let them feel that you really care about what they are trying to communicate.

Look at our Beloved Baba. When a student or adult talks to Swami in darshan, Sai sometimes leans closer to hear, and gives all His attention to the speaker. Giving our full attention to another who is speaking to us is an act of love. If you cannot stop what you are doing at the time, then communicate this and tell them when you will have the time to talk. When we stop what we are doing, and make eye contact, our gestures communicate this message: "I'm interested in what you have to say." This acknowledgment and recognition when we communicate to others is letting them know we care.

Swami guides us through our various stages of identity from birth to death. This helped me to understand that when the significant person in our life changes, the probable cause is our evolving natures. We are forced by nature to detach even though we may feel we are not ready.

Swami says, *"When you are born, your parents come first. Then comes peers; peers first, parents last. Then comes marriage; peers last, marriage partner first. Then Children come first; marriage partner last. Then comes job and career; child last. Soon old age, and you've had no time to think of God."*

Isn't this true concerning all of us as we go from infant to adult? When our children are little, how they adore their parents. Do we need to encourage them to communicate to us? NO. We usually cannot stop them from talking to us. We are the center of their life. When they begin school, they gradually, more and more begin to identify with their peers. Parents become last. The older they become the more they identify with their friends over their parents. This is why it is dangerous for them to keep bad company. They will confide in their friends rather than their parents, especially as they grow older. It is the parents' job to keep the line of communication open, even when they may want to shut it down. After their marriage, it is no longer the parents' responsibility to communicate with their children in the same way. Now it is a spouse's duty.

With time parents play a lesser and lesser role in the lives of their children. Your place of importance depends on their stage in life. Swami also said that when the parents feel less accepted by their own children, they then turn to money, fame and career. Hopefully this will help us to understand what is happening as our children evolve.

I spoke on respect in the last chapter. One of the major ways we violate the value of respect is with our speech.

Sometimes our words are correct, but our tone of voice is threatening. Tone is equally as important as the message. Respect is a value that is communicated through our whole presence: our thoughts, words, and deeds. We are too often disrespectful to each other when we communicate. You hear parents yelling at the children, giving authoritarian orders, not listening, insisting and criticizing, and then with anger. You find the children mimicking the same thing. Verbal abuse abounds in our culture today; we err with our tongue.

Sai says, *The eye commits only one sin, which is seeing bad things. The ear commits only one sin, which is listening to bad things. However, the tongue commits four sins. It speaks untruths, blames others, carries tales about others, and talks too much."* Summer Showers 1978 pg. 185

As parents, we know that we and our children abuse one another with speech. Many times we try to communicate with our teens and they want no part of it. When this happens it is very frustrating to both parties. When our children are verbally abusive, as parents we must not accept it. As I said in the last chapter, we are the parent and need to set a good example. If we become angry and respond by screaming, we continue to teach them this method of interaction which discourages communication, present and future.

If you get angry, Swami tells us what to do.

He says,      *"1. Remove yourself from the place of anger*
              *2. Drink a cold glass of water*
              *3. Lay down*
              *4. Look at yourself in the mirror (it will make you laugh)"*

Dr. Art-ong Jumsai scientifically explained the reasons for these steps. When you leave the place of anger, you walk out of the energy field. Staying in the same spot supports your anger. Drinking cold water, cools down the blood, and when you lay down, anger cannot rise up the spine. You can observe that when a seated person gets angry, he stands up.

If you are emotionally upset and not prepared to speak, then follow Swami's advice and cool down. Sometimes when angry, I would have to do all four steps. The very first step of walking away is especially critical because the angry energy is surrounding and influencing you. I would go to my bedroom to talk to Swami and think.

If I lost control with one of my children or spouse, when I was calm, I would admit that I was wrong, tell them I was sorry and that I would make every effort not do it again. Our family members can accept our weakness and mistakes when we speak the truth from our heart. When we are in denial, it creates a serious problem.

Sai Baba says, *"See how Nature adheres to truth. By God's command, the regularity of the seasons happen through the rule of law and orderly orbital gravitation. Man, too, has to learn this truth and live accordingly, with a heart attuned to truth and a mind saturated with love. Speech must be the flow of truth. Truth must be revered as one's very breath. The 'triple purity': speech free from pollution and falsehood, a mind free from the taint of passionate desire or hatred, and a body free from the poison of violence, this has to be attained by all."* Discourse December 5, 1985

We are all human, trying our best to overcome our weaknesses with Sai Baba guiding us. Why do we have such a difficult time admitting that we made a mistake? Is it not our ego, our fear and pride? We fear rejection if we allow others to think we are less than what our image projects. Doesn't our ego want us to look good sometimes at any cost?

Sai says, *"It is only fear that makes people warp the face of truth, to make it pleasant for those whom they fear."* Discourse October 19, 1966

Do we really think that we are faultless? If we are faultless we would not be here. When <u>we hurt</u> someone in our family, if we can admit our mistakes (because we are human) and earnestly make an effort to improve ourselves, these are valuable lessons for our children to learn. It teaches them how to resolve conflicts in their own relationships, and they will carry this learning with them into their own marriage and family or wherever they go.

Swami says, *"Let men and women consider others' mistakes to be small, however big they may be. Consider your own faults to be big, however small they may be. It is of utmost importance that you see the flaws in yourself, and eliminate them."* SS Ladies' Day Discourse November 19, 1995

Example: Mother says to teenage daughter. "Mary, I had a terrible day, the car broke down on the highway, the car bill was unexpected, and I'm not feeling well. I lost control when we talked. Please understand, I'm not angry with you, I love you very much. I'm so sorry that I lost control and screamed at you. I will make every effort not to have this happen again. Please accept my apology. I have this problem with loosing my temper. I'm working on it, and hopefully Sai will help me to control my anger before I hurt others. Can we at another time sit down and talk about the differences that we have?"

With an apology, as in the above example, how can anyone not forgive you? You are speaking your truth. This type of communication is very important.

Sai Baba says, *"Whatever news you receive about any event, you should receive it with calmness and serenity. If you get angry or irritated, you are losing your peace of mind. Stick to your own truth and be true to your own nature. Peace has to be realized through love. The world has to be brought back on to the rails, and it is love and peace alone which can achieve this. There may be people who hate us, but love them too. Develop forbearance, patience, peace and love, and carry on your work. This is true devotion."* Discourse December 9, 1985

We know that some people find admission of faults and apologies much easier to say than others. Parents know the family members who communicate more easily. When communication was more difficult for one member of the family, I would try to help them along after we have had time to calm down and think.

For example. "I see that you are upset. Did you have a bad day? (You may only get a nod but that's good.) I want to help you, I love you so much and do not like to see you upset. Can you tell me the problem?"

If the person tells you the problem by sharing his thoughts and/or feelings, then you can help him to understand his response to it. Many times there is not a solution to the problem, but if we can help our children get in touch with their reaction to a situation, it relieves the stress. Just the recognition of what is happening can help them feel less alone and give them peace.

Sai Baba says, *"We aspire for peace and comfort all the time, but where can we find it? Is it to be found in the material world around us? Experience shows that the peace and happiness to be got from external objects is not enduring. It is like a mirage which cannot quench the thirst. There can be no happiness without peace, but such peace can only be got through achieving equal-mindness on all occasions, whether one is subjected to pleasure or pain, praise or blame, gain or loss."* Discourse December 9, 1985

When we stand in the sun, our body makes a shadow. What happens when we walk away from the shadow? It follows us. What happens when we walk towards the shadow? It disappears. The same principel applies with admitting our hidden fears, faults, hurts, thoughts and feelings. They can disappear through acknowledgment. But if we walk away, they follow us and when we deny them and shove them down and away from childhood to adulthood, they stack up in layers because they have not been wiped clear with loving acceptance. When they stack too high, and there is no more room in your sub-conscious closet, the stuff overflows in anger and resentment.

The basic problem is that we are hurting ourselves by hiding our issues inside through denial. They begin to eat away at our self-esteem, like a mouse gnawing on a piece of cheese,—small nibbles, but oh, so annoying'. Finally our guilt cannot stand it any longer, and we explode in anger, just like an earthquake when there is too much pressure inside the earth. Our sub-conscious is like the earth; if we put too much pollution inside, the pressure builds up, we split open, and the garbage comes out in rage or some form of hysteria. All we have to do to prevent this from happening is to empty our garbage bin regularly by taking daily inventory of ourselves. Through communication with the key of love, you can prevent this from happening to yourselves or your spouse and child.

Sai Baba tells us, *"The easiest habit is to speak the truth. Love a person, and you no longer need to deceive him or her with a lie; you will feel that person deserves the truth, and nothing less than the truth. It saves a lot of bother."* Discourse March 3, 1958

Communication is two way. When one partner, be it a spouse or child, will not communicate their feelings or thoughts, and verbal resolution becomes impossible, let go. Continue to be loving and to pray. This is always helpful for all parties.

Sai Baba says, *"Truth is the current and Love is the bulb that it has to illumine."* Discourse May 12, 1968

Communication can also be a language of action and gestures. This we observe in our children. When they will not voice their inner thoughts, you can replay their actions with words in an effort to help them communicate with you.

For example: an unhappy face on a child, a moody, hanging head, the eyes avoiding contact are all unspoken messages to you. You can say, "You seem so unhappy, are you feeling bad today?" Sooner or later this will bring about a response; don't worry, it will eventually come out. Gentle love is a healing balm that comforts others, and whether they communicate their problem or not, they will feel your heartfelt love. Surround them with this love energy by visualizing light all around and within them.

As we did, our children often have unhappy experiences in their school. The children today call each other names, embarrass, humiliate and mock one another. Students can be so cruel, especially in the formation of exclusive clicks which insult or abuse those not included or rejected (from their roster.) They flaunt their "superiority" while imposing inferiority on outsiders. It is the same old game of "I'm better than you."

Sai says, *"Be vigilant about words. Slip while walking, the injury can be repaired, but slip while talking, the injury is irreparable."*

This makes us all feel badly whether we are adults or children. We, as adults, understand the game and our self-esteem hopefully is more established, but our children are more vulnerable. Many, many times they will not tell us about these insults because it hurts too much. But we can always make an effort, especially to watch for the signs of withdrawal or negative behaviour. They want to be accepted and loved but do not understand that often the people they want to associate with cannot give what they themselves also need and desire.

Sai says, *"Everyone should respect all others as one's own kin, having the same divine Spark and the same Divine Nature. Now, love and respect based on the innate Divinity are absent, so there is exploitation, deceit, greed and cruelty. When people become aware that all men are 'cells' of the Divine Body, then there will be no more devaluation of man. Man is a diamond; but he is now being treated by other men and by himself as a piece of glass."* Discourse April 1, 1975

How easy it is to criticize ourselves and others! The little judge inside of us just loves to judge others, instead of ourselves. It judges others appearance, habits, work, behaviour etc., etc.,

etc. The irony is that we ourselves hate to be criticized by others, and yet most of us criticize so often it is a national pastime.

Some examples: "You're late for dinner, you never called." "Just do it, don't ask why." "Don't you have something better to wear?" "You call this cleaning a room?" "Are you stupid, just look at this report?"

These, remember, are like waving a red flag in front of a bull! They are harsh and argumentative. Immediately, you want to start defending yourself and usually this is done by insulting the other person. We have to ask ourselves, "What purpose is this going to accomplish? How will this solve any problem? What will happen as a result of putting each other down?"

Our ego is involved when we chastise others. We have a need to feel more important. If there is a problem that needs to be addressed with a spouse or child, it can be done in a mature manner rather than an accusing and blaming one. We need to speak privately, calmly, and with steady love.

Example. Let's say your child got a very low grade on his/her report card. "Jim, I see that you got an F in English. Do you know why?" "No", he replies. "Would you like to think about it and we'll talk in an hour?" (always set a deadline) If the child wants to explore his/her own reasons, good. If they still have no answer for you then or later, you start asking questions.

"Jim, I really care about you and want to help you. I am going to ask you some questions to see where the problem is and then we can work together to solve it. Do you think this is a difficult subject? How often do you study this subject? Did you receive poor grades regularly on your English papers during this semester, or is this a recent development?"

If you pursue a line of questions that are not "put downs" or judgments, you will give the child an opportunity to answer, instead of defending themselves. After you question the child and determine a method to correct whatever allowed this incident to happen, you will need to monitor the correction or situation.

You continue, "We will work together three nights a week on English. I will expect you to show me your English homework before and after it is graded. I will call your teacher in a few weeks to see if she thinks you are improving and do whatever else is necessary to help you be the best that you can be."

Sai says, *"Even if you cannot oblige, at least you can speak obligingly. This means that you have to cleanse your speech of cynicism and satire and be ever sincere and sweet."* SSS # 10 pg. 281

After we judge others, and criticize, we like to talk about it...gossip. Women have been traditionally known as gossips, but men do as well. They gossip about people at work, politics, and organizations to which they belong. It is a bad habit, and serves no purpose except to bring attention to ourselves. We know something that others may not know. It is the boasting ego.

One year when we stayed with Swami, I sat on a chair, the same one everyday. The lady next to me was talking and a Seva Dal told her Swami was coming and not to talk. The lady responded, "This can't wait, it's a hot item!!!!" and continued her story.

One day, a man was listening to two other men talking about someone. He did not talk but only listened. Swami came up to him during darshan, asked and responded, *"Do you know what ABC means? Always Be in Good Company."* Swami knew just before darshan that he was listening to gossip. We are in error, listening to or speaking gossip. Spreading rumors about others is hurting their reputation, as well as harming ourselves.

We need to be ever so vigilant with our speech. The tongue is the most difficult sense to control, its tasting as well as its speech. When we see God in all beings, we would never wish to harm or hurt them with the spoken word.

Communication is the lifeline between family members; if it gets clogged up then there is little chance for domestic harmony, no air to breathe. We suffocate. Swami once told Dr. Hislop, "If you argue with your wife, do not go to sleep until the problem is solved." The same medicine can be applied to the children.

Swami says, *"The tongue has the extra power to harm and hurt, so you must exercise control over it. Do not pain anyone through your words; spread Love; be full of love. If you cannot love man, how can you hope to love God?"* SSS #8 pg. 31

## CHAPTER 18
# PARENTS' LOVE

*"When Love illumines thought, Truth is revealed.*

*When Love motivates action, it is transformed into Right Conduct.*

*When Love saturates feelings, it becomes calm and serene and ensures Peace*

*When anger, envy, greed and hate are cast away, Love dawns in  understanding and Non-Violence reigns supreme."*

Sai Baba

Dear students, young adults, newlyweds, moms, dads, and grandparents: writing this book has been an adventure with Sai Baba for me.  To be able to share Sai with anyone is His great gift.

I am profoundly aware of the hardship and challenge as well as the  grace that is given to parents by Sai Baba.  He loves you so very much.  How often He has said, *"Take one step toward me, and I will take 100 towards you.  Shed one tear for me; and I will shed 100 for you. I have the love of 1000 mothers."*

We grandparents are more gifted with knowledge in our old age, and have less opportunity to use it.  If I could be a parent today I would have changed many things.  But the gift I received from Swami is the ability to share what I have learned from Him with all you readers. I am eternally grateful.

I used to tell my family that the world outside our home can sometimes be less than kind. But inside our home, we should find a loving sanctuary, a place of refuge to go for understanding, caring, kindness, respect and above all, love. Our hearts are the altar and our homes, the church, for worshipping God. God lives within each of us. Children find God through their parents, and parents find the expression of God in each other.

Why should we continue to hurt one another? The world gives us enough pain. Must we inflict more on each other! I think not.

Forgiveness is the virtue that allows us to continue our relationships even though we have hurt one another. Hurting each other is part of the grand play. We do it out of ignorance. We do it because we ,ourselves, have hurt ourselves and hurt so much. We do it to get even. How foolishly we act. We hold grudges that will eventually eat us alive, and for what reason? To hurt each other, but in reality who is hurting whom? Everything comes back to us.

If God can forgive the greatest sinner in the world, why can we not do the same? **When we learn to forgive others, we can learn to forgive ourselves.**

Sai Baba says, *"Love lives by giving and forgiving; self lives by getting and forgetting."*

Love is so generous, it can accept and heal the faults, the ignorance, the past errors, the fears, the emotional scars, the trappings that pollute our minds. The heart is God's home, and if we live in His divine home, we will bring His light, joy, happiness and love into the hearts and minds of our family. We mothers have this duty in common. We are responsible for representing God in our family. It is our divine nature and duty. We can sacrifice more than men as we have been given this gift from God: our feminine nature.

Sai says, *"The spirit of sacrifice that is expressed while doing service is only found in mothers. When a mother watches somebody shedding tears, her eyes get wet too. Women have so much kindness in them."* Sathya Sai Newsletter Summer 1996 pg. 6

Be glad to be a woman, the job that God has assigned to us in this life is inferior to none. It is a challenge stretching human ability, to raise a child in this world of negativity. God must march beside us, and we must know He is constantly arranging everything for us. Just to know that He is comforting, instructing, healing and holding us in His arms, is reward enough.

You have a job to do parents, that is humanly improbable but divinely possible. The effort that you make will determine the grace that He showers. Don't be overwhelmed nor threatened by the content of this book. Start slowly and arrive safely.

Each child is different, each child is unique, each child comes with different karma, each child has gifts to offer and challenges to be met. They are like clay that needs to be sculptured into a work of art by your loving hands. Treat them as delicate flowers. See them as an opportunity for growth and promotion in the spiritual quest which is none other than self-realization. They are our chance to share God's love. They are our great fortune to serve God. They are our lessons to be learned.

If a man and woman, husband and wife, mother and father cannot heal their relationship, then this unhealed attitude will live within your child. It is the sin of not forgiving that is passed down from generation to generation. Somewhere along the line of heritage the cord must be severed. Who has the strength to cut it with love? Knowing that God is here beside and among us in living form, can we not heal our relationships and change our behaviour? Walk forward husbands and wives; strengthen your relationship with one another, which strengthens your contact with the God within you. See the God in each other, not the weakness. When you have removed the deciding injury, your children will feel your love and blossom into excellence.

There is no other way than the way that He has expressed in the pages of this book. We can fight it, ignore it or do nothing, but He will always prevail. Eventually in this life or another, we will have to surrender to His divine will. With this in mind, why struggle? Why wait? Make it happen in this life. Follow His teachings, and call upon Him for help, moment to moment.

His Love will never let us down. Trust that He has given us this family for a divine purpose. Not even a blade of grass sways in the breeze without the will of God. If He cares for the blade of grass, will He not give us the same consideration? Yes, God certainly loves us more than we love ourselves. This is His challenge, making us aware of His Love for us, so we can love ourselves. This is the transformation we truly crave: heart to heart. When we connect with His Love, it flows to all the family members, nourishing and nurturing them.

We travel great distances to Prasanthi to see God and feel His love. He recharges us and sends us back into the world to be His beacon lights flickering in the dark corners of the world. We can use this same process in our home, which is our family's shrine. We, too, can cleanse, heal and energize the little batteries of our children with love. Swami is our sterling example of perfect parenting, one to emulate with our own children.

Everything Sai Baba does holds a message for us, has meaning. He, our divine parent, is our example. If you are in doubt as to what to do, analyze how He works with you and with His students. It is no different with us and our children.

The knowledge, the challenge, and His love exist within you. There is nothing more for me to add, except.........I love you, too.

Sai Baba says, *"In every discourse Swami speaks about love. How many practise it? Who has this love? Love is not to be seen anywhere."* SS Christmas Discourse 1997

*"It is said that love has no form. But love has a form. The mother who loves her child, expresses the form of love."* SS January 1998

# BIBLIOGRAPHY

◊ Buzzell, Keith. *The Children of Cyclops: The Influence of Television Viewing on the Developing Human Brain.* 1998 California: AWSNA.

◊ Everett, Miles. *How Television Poisons Children's Minds.* 1997 California: Miles Publishing.

◊ Fischer, Paul. "Brand Logo Recognition by Children Aged 3 to 6 Years: Mickey Mouse and Old Joe the Camel" JAMA Vol. 266, No. 22 December 11, 1991

◊ Gross, Liza. "Current Risks: Experts finally link Electromagnetic Fields and Cancer, " SIERRA, May/June

◊ Johnson, Susan. "TV and Our Chinldren's Minds". Spring 1999 pages: Gudolf Steiner College

◊ Healy, Jane. *Endangered Minds: Why children Don't Think and What We Can Do About It.* 1990 New York: Simon and Schuster

◊ Mander, Jerry. *Four Arguments for the Elimination of Television.* 1978 New York: William Morrow and Co.

◊ Pearce, Joseph Chilton. *Evolution's End: Claiming the Potential of Our Intelligence.* 1992 California: Harper San Francisco.

◊ Poplawski, Thomas. "Losing Our Sense". Renewal: A Journal for Waldorf Education, Vol. 7, No. 2, Fall 1998

◊ Scheidler, Thomas. "Television, Video Games and the LD Child". 1995 Pamphlet: Greenwood Institute.

◊ Singer, Dorothy. "Caution: Television May Be Hazardous to a Child's Mental Health". Developmental and Behavioral Pediatrics, Vol. 10, No. 5, October 1989.

◊ Soesman, Albert. *The Twelve Senses: Wellsprings of the Soul.* 1998 England: Hawthorn Press.

◊ Tiller, William. "Robust Manifestations of Subtle Energies in Physical Reality and Its Implications for Future Medicine". Lecture, Stanford University, April 28th, 1999.

◊ Winn, Marie. *The Plug-in Drug.* 1985 New York Penguin Books.

◊ Zuckerman, Diana M. and Barry S. Zuckerman. "Television's Impact on Children". Pediatrics, Vol. 75, No. 2, 1985

**Reference to Swami's quotes.**
SSS means Sathya Sai Speaks Series of Books
SS means Sanathana Sarathi

SRI SATHYA SAI BOOKS AND
PUBLICATIONS TRUST PRASANTHI NILAYAM
PIN 515134, ANANTAPUR DISTRICT,
ANDHRA PRADESH, INDIA.
IMPORTER / EXPORTER CODE NO. 0990001032
RESERVE BANK OF INDIA EXPORTER CODE NO. HS-2001198

**THE VAHINI SERIES : (BOOKS WRITTEN BY BHAGAVAN SRI SATHYA SAI BABA.)**

Bhagavatha Vahini ................................................................. 30.00
(The story of the Glory of the Lord)
Dharma Vahini (The Path of virtue and Marality) ..................... 13.00
Dhyana Vahini (The Practice of Meditarion) ........................... 13.00
Geetha Vahini (The Divine Gospel) ....................................... 21.00
Jnana Vahini (The Stream of Eternal Wisdom) ........................ 12.00
Leela Kaivalya Vahini (The Cosmic Play of God) ..................... 12.00
Prasanthi Vahini (The Supreme Bliss of Divine) ...................... 12.00
Prasnothara Vahini (Answers to Spiritual Questions) .............. 12.00
Prema Vahini (The Stream of Divine Love) ............................. 13.00
Rama Katha Rasa Vahini Part - I. ......................................... 38.00
(The Sweet Story of Rama's Glory)
Rama Katha Rasa Vahini Part-II ............................................ 27.00
(The Sweet Story of Rama's Glory)
Sandeha Nivarini (Clearance of Spiritual Doubts) ................... 16.00
Sathay Sai Vahini (Spiritual Message of Sri Sathya Sai) ......... 25.00
Sutra Vahini (Analytical Aphorism on Supreme Reality) ........... 12.00
Upanishad Vahini (Essence of Vedic Knowledge ..................... 15.00
Vidya Vahini (Flow of Spiritual Eudcation) ............................. 14.00

**SATHYA SAI SPEAKS SERIES : (DISCOURSES BY BHAGAVAN SRI SATHYA SAI BABA) (REVISED & ENLARGED EDITIONS)**

Sathya Sai Speaks Vol. I      (Year  1953 to 1960) ................. 29.00
Sathya Sai Speaks Vol. II     (Year  1961 to 1962) ................. 40.00
Sathya Sai Speaks Vol. III    (Year  1963) ............................. 35.00
Sathya Sai Speaks Vol. IV     (Year  1964) ............................. 34.50
Sathya Sai Speaks Vol. V      (Year  1965) ............................. 43.00
Sathya Sai Speaks Vol. VI     (Year  1966) ............................. 45.00
Sathya Sai Speaks Vol. VII    (Year  1967) ............................. 47.00
Sathya Sai Speaks Vol. VIII   (Year  1968) ............................. 35.00
Sathya Sai Speaks Vol. IX     (Year  1969) ............................. 30.00
Sathya Sai Speaks Vol. X      (Year  1970) ............................. 36.50
Sathya Sai Speaks Vol. XI     (Year  1971 to 1972) ................. 51.00
Sathya Sai Speaks Vol. XII    (Year  1973 to 1974) ................. 42.00
Sathya Sai Speaks Vol. XIII   (Year  1975 to 1977) ................. 34.00
Sathya Sai Speaks Vol. XIV    (Year  1978 to 1980) ................. 45.00
Sathya Sai Speaks Vol. XV     (Year  1981 to 1982) ................. 47.00
Sathya Sai Speaks Vol. XVI    (Year  1983) ............................. 30.00
Sathya Sai Speaks Vol. XVII   (Year  1984) ............................. 31.00
Sathya Sai Speaks Vol. XVIII  (Year  1985) ............................. 30.00
Sathya Sai Speaks Vol. XIX    (Year  1986) ............................. 44.00
Sathya Sai Speaks Vol. XX     (Year  1987) ............................. 40.00
Sathya Sai Speaks Vol. XXI    (Year  1988) ............................. 40.00
Sathya Sai Speaks Vol. XXII   (Year  1989) ............................. 40.00
Sathya Sai Speaks Vol. XXIII  (Year  1990) ............................. 55.00
Sathya Sai Speaks Vol. XXIV   (Year  1991) ............................. 63.00
Sathya Sai Speaks Vol. XXV    (Year  1992) ............................. 50.00

- by Rita Bruce
**FOR SALE ONLY IN INDIA**

Transformation of the Heart - by Judy Warner ..........................25.00
Reconnecting the Love Energy ...............................................25.00
- by Phyllis Krystal
Taming our Monkey Mind - by Phyllis Krystal ..........................35.00
Suggestions for Study Groups and Individuals
use of the Ceiling on Desires Programme ...............................10.00
A Catholic Priest Meets Sai Baba .........................................40.00
- by Don Mario Mazzoleni
Pathways to God - by Jonathan Roof......................................34.00

## INLAND / OVERSEAS BOOK ORDERS & SUBSCRIPTION OFR MONTHLY MAGAZINE SANATHANA SARATHI

Books are despatched by Regd. Book Post only subject to availability. Indents and remittences within India should be received by Money Order/Indian Postal Order/Acccount Payee Cheques/Bank Drafts.

### REMITTANCES

Remittances from Overseas toward Book Orders/Sanathana Sarathi Subscriptions (English & Telugu) can be sent by A/C payee Bank cheque/Demand Draft/International Money Order in **FOREIGN CURRENCY ONLY AND NOT IN INDIAN RUPEES.** Sending Cash Currency is liable to be confiscated by Government.

All remittences should be in favour of **THE CONVENER, SRI SATHYA SAI BOOKS AND PUBLICATIONS TRUST, PRASANTHI NILAYAM, ANANTHAPUR DISTRICT, ANDHRA PRADESH, INDIA, PIN CODE - 515134,** payable at State Bank of India, Prasanthi Nilayam (Branch Code No. 2786) mentioning full address in capitals with Area Pin Code, Zip Code No., where the books are to be despatched.

### POSTAGE (INLAND)

At the rate of 50 paise per 100 gms plus Registration charges Rs. 14/- For an order of 1 kg parcel, postage Rs. 5/- (+) Regn. charges Rs. 14/- total Rs. 19/- For 2 kgs parcel Rs. 24/- For 3 kgs parcle Rs. 29/- For 4 kgs parcel Rs. 34/- and for 5 Kgs parcel Rs. 39/- While remitting, please calculate the cost of the books indented (+) postage (+) Registration charges.

### POSTAGE (OVERSEAS)

| | |
|---|---|
| 1 kg parcel | Rs. 60.00 |
| 2 kg parcel | Rs. 78.00 |
| 3 kg parcel | Rs. 110.00 |
| 4 kg parcel | Rs. 140.00 |
| 5 kg parcel | Rs. 172.00 |

(Packing and Forwarding charges Rs. 20.00 per packet extra)